For as long as I've known Ally, she's been trying to convince me that I'm a writer—and I have to admit I'm still a bit skeptical about that. But if anyone could get me to write something, it would be her! If you're skeptical that you're a writer, she can get you to write too. All you have to do is read this book.

Amy Brown, cohost of *The Bobby Bones Show* and host of the *4 Things with Amy Brown* podcast

Ally has a rare and unique gift for helping others rediscover and share vital parts of themselves through the written word. As a longtime professional in the mental wellness space, I deeply respect the time she invested in gaining such an understanding of the psychological benefits of writing. I've personally experienced her transformational process, and her strength and wisdom shine in this powerful resource.

Miles Adcox, CEO of Onsite

Ally has written the book many of us need right now. With a perfect blend of grace and practicality, she grabs your hand and leads you into what will become a life-changing and lifelong practice of writing it all down. I don't think anyone is more qualified to be your guide through his process of building a new habit and forging new paths and possiilities for your life.

Hannah Brencher, author of *Fighting Forward* and *Come Matter Here*

*Power of Writing It Down* is a book that speaks to the heart of why ing is so important for everyone and motivates us to do it. I've had leasure of working with Ally on numerous occasions, and each I've been challenged and encouraged to stretch my writing chops O FOR IT! This book provides a framework for recognizing that have a story to tell and will help you develop the skills to tell To all writers or future writers out there: this is the book you've iting for from the guide who cares, the guide you can trust.

Kim Gravel, entrepreneur and TV personality

I talk to people all the time who want to write their story, or even to write a book, but most of them don't end up doing it. What they need in order to get started is simple: a little bit of direction, a lot of inspiration, and a reminder that they are the writer they know themselves to be! This book provides all of that and more. If you want to write but aren't sure where to start, this is the book for you.

Bob Goff, *New York Times* bestselling
author and Chief Balloon Inflator

Nothing in my life has served me more than writing down my stor
When you write down your story, you tell yourself what it means a
why it matters. But writing down your story isn't easy. Finally, a terr
book that tells you how.

Donald Miller, author of *Business Made S*

Good things come to those who write. I'm thrilled that this b
help so many people benefit from the power of putting wor
page, learning through Allison Fallon's firm but friendly
both why and how to develop their own writing practi
words can change everything.

Anne Bogel, author of *D*
*It*, host of the *What Shou*
podcast, and creator of *Mo*

Ally Fallon is remarkable. Simply and elegantl
is always interested in things that can expand
the humanity to offer help to those who can b
tiful mind. Ally is a great human being and w
has learned and experienced to help those
excellence.

Scott Hamilton, author ar

*The*
writ
the p
time,
and C
we all
yours.
been w

After reading just the first few sentences of this book, I felt seen, understood, and even equipped by Allison. She pairs empathy and emotional intelligence with practical tools to help you grow as a human. Folks from all industries and backgrounds will get value out of this book.

Joanna Waterfall, founder of Yellow Co.

I always knew I had a story to share, but the idea of writing an entire book seemed daunting. When I got a book deal, Ally helped me take an overwhelming job and break it into manageable pieces. Before I knew it, I was holding my book in my hands. The process that made me an author is the exact process she outlines in this book. If you have a story to share, you need to read this.

Caitlin Crosby, founder and
CEO of The Giving Keys

*The Power of Writing It Down* literally saved my life. I went from panic attacks and chronic burnout to letting Ally guide me through the process she outlines in this book. I've come back to life again through these steps, and I know you will, too.

Melody Miles, author and founder of Soulcation

In this book, Ally offers a path for us to bear witness to our lives through the practice of writing. Her wisdom, practical advice, and encouraging words give readers the tools needed to start writing in order to find their own unique voice and to live more fulfilled lives. Ally shows us we all have a story to tell, and our story matters.

Amy J Brown, cohost of the *Take Heart*
podcast and Prepare to Publish graduate

# The Power of Writing It Down

# The Power of Writing It Down

A Simple Habit to Unlock Your Brain and Reimagine Your Life

ALLISON FALLON

ZONDERVAN
THRIVE

ZONDERVAN THRIVE

*The Power of Writing It Down*

Requests for information should be addressed to:
Zondervan, 3900 *Sparks Dr. SE, Grand Rapids, Michigan* 49546

Zondervan titles may be purchased in bulk for educational, business, fundraising, or sales promotional use. For information, please email SpecialMarkets@Zondervan.com.

ISBN 978-0-310-35936-4 (audio)

---

Library of Congress Cataloging-in-Publication Data

Names: Fallon, Allison, author.
Title: The power of writing it down : a simple habit to unlock your brain and reimagine your life / Allison Fallon.
Description: Grand Rapids : Zondervan, 2020. | Includes bibliographical references. | Summary: "For anyone feeling stuck and looking to make sense of life, author and writing coach Allison Fallon shares a simple practice and proven method to reclaiming your narrative, increasing your emotional and spiritual health, and discovering more clarity and freedom in The Power of Writing It Down"—Provided by publisher.
Identifiers: LCCN 2020029304 (print) | LCCN 2020029305 (ebook) | ISBN 9780310359340 (hardcover) | ISBN 9780310359357 (ebook)
Subjects: LCSH: Writing—Psychological aspects. | Behavior modification. | Written communication.
Classification: LCC BF456.W8 F35 2020 (print) | LCC BF456.W8 (ebook) | DDC 158.1/6—dc23
LC record available at https://lccn.loc.gov/2020029304
LC ebook record available at https://lccn.loc.gov/2020029305

---

The author is represented by Bryan Norman of Alive Literary Agency, www.aliveliterary.com.

Zondervan Thrive, an imprint of Zondervan, publishes books that empower readers with insightful, expert-driven ideas for a life of thriving in today's world.

*Cover design: Curt Diepenhorst*
*Cover photography: Thomas Vogel | Getty Images*
*Interior design: Denise Froehlich*

*Printed in the United States of America*

---

20 21 22 23 24 /LSC/ 10 9 8 7 6 5 4 3 2 1

*To my clients and friends who have braved the path of "writer" already. And to those who are yet to come. May your words shape you, your community, and the world in ways you never dreamed possible. May it deepen your courage and strengthen your inspiration.*

*May you never forget the sound of your own voice.*

# Contents

CHAPTER 1

# Something to Express

## You have something to express. This book can help you discover it.

Most people go their whole lives without ever truly expressing themselves. We have stories to tell, ideas to share, dreams of the future, visions and versions of ourselves that want permission to live and breathe in the physical world, but we won't let them. Instead, we silently coach ourselves to sit down, follow the rules, be more reasonable, tend to our responsibilities, and keep the peace.

What is the cost of *holding back* what is trying to be expressed through you?

The most immediate cost is the way you feel in your physical body, right now. It might be a general sense of dread or boredom. A feeling like you don't want to get out of your bed and live your life today. Sure, you'll do it. You always do. You're a disciplined person with a good work ethic. And you have people counting on you. You can't let them down. But at the end of every day, and even at the beginning, you have this strange and looming sense that something is not right. Let's call that feeling *The Hang-Up*.

I call it *The Hang-Up* because it's usually the one thing that doesn't quite make sense in a sea of other things that seem perfectly reasonable and ordinary. You've got a pretty good life, no better or worse than anyone else's. You're smart, you tell yourself. You have a plan and a proven path forward, and it's probably best to just stay the course. So you ignore that gentle suggestion from deep in your gut that things are not quite right. You remind yourself there are people in the world with far worse problems, and you tell yourself that what you need, more than anything, is an attitude adjustment. Maybe you should make a list of the things you're grateful for. What a totally reasonable, measured, responsible, and mature thing to do. But what if what you need is something you haven't quite put your finger on yet?

Since you're holding this book in your hands, I want you to consider something with me. What if *The Hang-Up* doesn't have anything to do with a bad attitude? What if it isn't a problem, and what if it doesn't mean something is wrong with you? What if *The Hang-Up* is more like a message trying to get your attention? What if it is begging for you to put words to it, to give it a name? What if it wants to have a *voice*?

What if it won't shut up until you listen?

I imagine you're probably thinking to yourself something along the lines of, *Okay, that's fine. I can learn to live with this. It's really not all that unpleasant. I just need to keep myself busy so that I don't notice it too much. And at night, when it's the worst, I'll watch TV and drink a few glasses of wine. That always does the trick. And when The Hang-Up gets even heavier, I'll smoke some pot, or pop a Xanax, or maybe look at some porn before I fall asleep.*

We all have infinite strategies to keep us from hearing our own voices.

There's a reason we do this. Because it's *unpleasant* at first to sit and listen, to learn to hear our own voices. It's confusing and, at times, infuriating. *The Hang-Up* feels like an unnecessary detour from an otherwise pretty-good life. When we listen to what it is telling us, it seems to be suggesting things that are terrifying or counterintuitive or just plain absurd. It's easier by a *long* shot to drink wine and watch TV than it is to try and figure out why this voice is urging us to quit the job, or set a new boundary in an old friendship, or let go of some stability or security that has for years or even decades given us peace.

What's trying to be expressed rarely makes sense in a logical way, and even when it does, the words it gives us and what they are suggesting we do next can shake us terribly. Even if we can find the courage to pay attention, what are we supposed to do with the resultant unrest?

So instead of listening, we try to outrun *The Hang-Up* altogether. We fill our lives with endless things that are fun and exciting and that look good on Instagram and that get us plenty of praise and attention.

"You're such a good mom!"

"Another award! Wow—congratulations!"

"You're so inspiring!"

"That *vacation*!"

But deep down, none of the attention or praise means much of anything because it is landing in the wrong place. It's all a big distraction from the main event, from what our souls are here to do. It's all disconnected from the most important, most valuable, most deeply enriching and satisfying thing you could ever own: your voice.

If what I've written so far makes no sense to you, I hate to say it, but you're not going to enjoy this book. But if what I've written here resonates with you on a deep level—even a level you don't understand quite yet—hang in there with me. I'm going to teach you a simple, easily accessible, and totally free tool you can use that is proven to help you *find your voice*. In doing so, you just might reclaim your life.

## The Power of Words

Words are powerful. In fact, I'd like to argue, words are one of the most powerful forces we have access to on this planet. This is why, as the creation myth goes, the God of the universe spoke the world into existence using nothing other than words. It's why a multi-billion-dollar industry (self-help) uses positive thoughts (read: words) to help us feel better, look better, and be better in our lives. It's why we hang on the words of leaders like Dr. Martin Luther King Jr. and C. S. Lewis and John Steinbeck and Mother Teresa and thousands of others.

This is why we read *words* at important occasions like weddings, and why we write words to friends to mark moments like birthdays and anniversaries. It's why yelling a curse word out the window at a passing driver would be considered an insult and why a friend of mine writes a short note to his wife every day before he leaves for work. He told me he wants her to know, down to her bones, that he loves her. That's the power of words.

Words can start a revolution or send a vital message to someone who desperately needs it. With a word, we can calm our own fears or the fears of someone we love. Words can change everything.

*He's not going to make it.*

*It's a girl.*

*You are beautiful.*

*I can't do this anymore.*

*We're going to be okay.*

Words are everything, yet most of us are not using them to their fullest potential or to our greatest advantage. Think about it: words are the *most* powerful tool we have to create the life we long for. Yet they are also often our most under-utilized resource. So why aren't we leveraging the power of words to bring about the life and the world we dream of for ourselves, for our neighbors, and for our children?

## The Change You're Looking For

Take a minute and think about something you'd like to change in your life or in the world. Maybe there's something relatively superficial. You want to lose ten pounds, get a small raise at work, or start flossing your teeth more regularly. Maybe it's something a little bit loftier. A dream or vision you want to bring to life—moving into a new home, finding your dream job, starting your own company, or starting a family.

Maybe the thing you want to change is far less tangible. Perhaps it's this nagging sense that something is "off" in your life. Maybe every morning, you wake up with a kind of low-grade anxiety and you wish you could feel more at peace with yourself. Maybe it's the way you feel in a certain relationship. Every time you try to talk to your spouse, or go home for Christmas, or try to get back in the dating scene, you feel the same deep dread. You wish it could be different. But no matter what you do, it doesn't ever change.

Maybe you're unlikely to find yourself obsessing about things in your own life you'd like to change. Perhaps, for you, the thoughts are more about how we can heal and change the world we're living in. Maybe your "thing" is online bullying or the addiction pandemic or the widespread violence of school shootings or racial discrimination or the pay gap between men and women. There is no shortage of problems to address or changes that need our attention.

Whatever you would like to see change in your life or in this world, you need to know that this impulse to change is deeply human. The drive to grow and change is natural and evolutionary. You'd be hard-pressed to find a human being who doesn't have something about themselves, their lives, their bodies or their environment that they wish was different.

You'll notice, as you think back to the last time you tried to change something about your life, your body, yourself, or your environment, the problem is that change doesn't come easily. In fact, we have a tendency to put an incredible amount of energy and effort into change without seeing much of a result. As you think about the last time you tried to change—*really* change something that mattered to you—ask yourself how many times you repeated the old behavior pattern from your past before the new pattern became second nature. Hundreds? Did it take years? Did it feel like a lifetime? Or perhaps you were never able to change the pattern at all.

Consider for a moment how many times you've started a new diet program, or started off a new year promising yourself you'd get to the gym more often, only to end the year at exactly the same weight and with exactly the same workout habits you've always had. It's almost like walking around the same block over and over again. You might think you're walking in a new direction. It might seem like you are at certain points. And then—darnit!—there's that same old tree all over again.

The word I hear people use the most often is *stuck*. I'm stuck in a rut, stuck in a toxic relationship, stuck in a self-destructive pattern, stuck in a job that makes me feel miserable, stuck in a city I hate, stuck in a world that tells me I'm worthless and I don't matter. Stuck. Stuck. Stuck.

Why is this? Is this because we're lazy? Undisciplined? Is it because we're not as committed to change as we think we are? I would argue that none of this is so. While these are often the reasons we find ourselves in the frustrating process of circling that same block over and over again, our lack of progress has nothing to do with our lack of effort. In fact, now that I've read the research I'm about to show you, I can tell you with surefire confidence that the reason we get stuck in negative patterns has nothing to do with willpower, discipline, goodwill, or our work ethic. It has everything to do with our brains.[1]

Our brains are remarkable organs that were designed with survival in mind. I am not a neuroscientist, but I've done just enough research on this topic to be dangerous, and here's my incredibly simplistic take: our brains have mastered the skill of *automating* behavior to make it as easy as possible. Think about it this way: when you take an action—or even think a thought, for that matter—a tiny little messenger is sent from one brain cell to another brain cell. It's almost like the messenger is saying, "This is how we take out the garbage," or "This is what we think about your mother-in-law."*

The *path* this message takes is called a neural pathway. The more times that path is traveled, the more well-worn it becomes. So when that little "messenger" has traveled the path 100 times or 1000 times or 10,000 times, it becomes well-worn enough that your brain doesn't even have to stop to think before you take out the trash or judge your mother-in-law. It just does it. You probably most easily recognize this tendency by your strange ability to drive to a place you lived a decade ago but haven't visited in years. Or how about remembering a friend's old phone number?

Your brain has automated this behavior.

From an evolutionary perspective, this is *brilliant*. Who needs to waste a bunch of time thinking about how to brush

---

* I actually adore my own mother-in-law (she's wonderful!). I only use this example because of the ubiquitous idea that mothers-in-law are difficult.

your teeth or make your mom's famous chocolate chip cookies? Who needs to recall, each time you see a person, how you feel about them? Nobody has time or energy for that when we have more important things to do.

But from the perspective of someone who is trying to change, grow, or evolve past the mistakes of their past, their family, or their ancestors, this is why we often feel ourselves bumping up against the "rut" of an old habit or pattern. Not because we're lazy or undisciplined people, but because we are, quite literally, fighting against the deep pathways that were carved in our brains a long time ago. You might be trying to change your path in earnest. But that little messenger in your brain says, *No thanks! I know the way to go.*

You don't need to understand all of the neuroscience or psychology of how your brain works right now. What you *do* need to understand is that you have a key to unlock the mystery of your brain, to jump out of those old ruts, to carve new pathways when you realize the old ones aren't taking you where you want to go anymore. In this book, I'm going to show you not only why writing is *the* tool to help you do this but also how writing can teach you to break old habits, reroute old pathways, and find a new way forward.

Even more than any of that, you need to know the sense you have, deep down, that a life full of joy and confidence is out there, and all the abundance you could possibly imagine *does* exist. It is not impossible. It is within your reach. The change you're looking for—the more peaceful, satisfying romantic partnership; the strong supportive friendships; the confidence to ask for what you want and need without apologizing; the resources to build a life filled with genuine bliss—these things are at your fingertips.

The question, of course, is, how do you get from a place of

*stuck* to a place of *bliss*? In this book, I'm going to teach you a simple, totally free practice anyone can use to get more of what they want.

You *can* stop circling that same block over and over again. It doesn't take more willpower, more discipline, or even all that much more time—most of which I know you don't have to give.

How?

Through the incredibly simple practice of *writing things down*.

## Why Writing It Down?

Most of us do not like to think about writing things down. The act of writing in and of itself has a stigma to it that keeps most of us from ever picking up a pen. Somewhere along the way, we picked up the idea that writing was reserved for a particularly talented or trained group of people, and we are not one of them. Of course, this doesn't make sense. Every day, you write a host of text messages, emails, grocery lists, birthday cards, Instagram captions, Facebook messages, Tweets, and who knows what else.

Writing is not some elite activity reserved for the uniquely gifted. Writing is communication, self-discovery, creativity, spirituality, and self-expression. Writing is the essential tool we use to find and practice our sense of voice. Writing is a distinctly human impulse. Why on earth should you be excluded from the practice?

Still, as a culture, for some reason we cling to this odd notion that writing is for some people and not for others. Even when we *want* to or have to write something—like a presentation for work, an Instagram caption, or an anniversary card—we still feel an almost physical resistance to sitting down and putting an actual pen to an actual piece of paper. We'll do almost anything not to have to *do* the writing.

Meanwhile, research shows that writing for as little as twenty minutes a day for four days in a row can measurably improve your mood. You might think to yourself, "Twenty minutes? That's a lot."

Is it a lot? Or is it our resistance to writing talking again? Sure, on one hand, twenty minutes out of a day that's already packed from morning to night with all kinds of good and important things *is* a lot. Especially if you have a job, or family responsibilities, or care about the people in your life and want to invest in them. Especially if you're a primary caregiver of young children, in which case your schedule is full of the not-so-simple logistics of human survival. No big deal.

So yes, twenty minutes is a lot.

But track with me here for a second. What if twenty minutes spent doing something like writing down your deepest thoughts and feelings might make everything else you do *easier*? What if it made it simple to turn down that lunch date you didn't want to accept in the first place—the one you're now rushing around for, the one about which you're feeling guilty because you don't want to go, because you're going against your better judgment, because you're going to be late and this person with whom you didn't really want to spend time is now waiting for you? What if writing made all of that easier?

What if twenty minutes of writing a day could make it easier to fall asleep at night, so you no longer lie awake for an hour, panicking about how you're going to pay your bills this month or about whether your oldest child is going to play soccer this year and how you're going to manage the game schedule with a new baby?

What if writing made it easier for you to articulate, in a way that did not infuriate your partner, exactly what you need from him or her so that you could finally make progress in that conversation you've tried to have too many times to count?

What if writing made your life easier because it reduced your anxiety, lifted you out of those brief moments of depression, clarified your vision, boosted your confidence, improved your immune system, and even made you less likely to visit the doctor? What if it clarified what really matters to you and made you feel like you're living your life on purpose? What if twenty minutes really turned into what felt like hours of time and copious energy added to every week?

Would it be worth it?

If you're skeptical, or if twenty minutes still sounds like a lot to you, that's fine. You're not alone. You can start with five minutes. Or two. Or start with one word scribbled on a scrap of paper somewhere. A little love note to yourself, or a bottle thrown out to sea as an SOS. A last-ditch effort to call something beyond you for help. You can start with what you have and then watch it grow into something much bigger than what you imagined under the law of increasing returns. The data shows this works, and so does my experience.

Whatever amount you give, you get more in return.

## What Writing Can Help Us Do:

1. Name our experience so we can more fully understand it.
2. Give language to the future we want to create so it stops feeling vague and begins to seem achievable.
3. Build a bridge (neural pathways) between the now we're experiencing and the future we'd like to create.
4. Heal and engineer our own resilience from past experience.
5. Find perspective for life's challenges, large and small.
6. Invent brand-new solutions for age-old problems.
7. Build our confidence.

8. Increase our working memory and overall cognitive power.
9. Cultivate more gratitude and contentment.
10. Provide clarity for our decisions.
11. Increase satisfaction in our romantic partnerships.
12. Level up our immune system, help us sleep better, etc.
13. Combat and curb anxiety, stress, and depression.
14. Tune out the well-meaning and critical voices around us so we can finally understand what we think.

You don't have to *feel* like a writer to use writing as a tool. Anyone can use writing as a tool to begin experiencing more meaning and joy in life, to overcome what were previously limitations and to begin to create positive change in the world. This book is going to teach you exactly how to do it.

## Why We Are Holding Back

I'm the founder of a company called Find Your Voice, which helps writers who don't know where to start. To "find your voice" involves finding your power, your *agency*, your ability to create something from nothing, the deep capacity you have to set in motion a change in your life or in the world around you. To find your voice means you begin to see yourself more clearly—who you are and what you're here for—and to have the strength and confidence to begin to *become* that empowered version of yourself in the physical world.

There are infinite resources to help you on this journey. Research shows that mediums like yoga, dance, breathwork, spirituality, prayer, music, writing, energy work, therapy, brain spotting, trauma work of all kinds, and body work are all deeply effective. But here's why I decided to focus on the tool of writing.

First, I meet people all the time who claim they love to write or want to write, but something is stopping them. Sometimes they have a book idea, or there's a screenplay they've been dreaming about. Other times it's as simple as an Instagram caption. "I want to share this photo of us, but I never know what to write," a friend told me—a friend who *always* has something insightful to say.

Why does the need to write a caption make it more difficult for my friend to share her photo? What is keeping her from sharing her thoughts? What keeps us from the words that connect us to ourselves, to the people we love, and to the world around us?

You might be thinking to yourself that this all sounds a little dramatic, considering we're talking about an Instagram caption, and you're right. But what is underneath the Instagram caption, from my view, is the pattern I'm getting at here—a pattern that is all too tragic and common: we *want* to express something, but we hold back. Why?

Is it possible that the very act of writing—expressing ourselves through the written word—could help us reach the full expression of ourselves? I believe the answer is yes, which is why I am writing this book.

Another reason I'm focusing on writing is that, despite all the mediums available to help us find our voices, most of us still don't have the first clue how to actually use those mediums to do it. We might *want* to find our true voices. We might find ourselves thinking about how we have something to offer the world that we haven't been able to articulate yet. Most of us flounder around, wondering what we're actually supposed to *do* to move in the right direction. When it comes to something as important and elusive as discovering my place in the world and what makes me matter, how do I make progress?

This book will help you answer that question. Not only that, but the answer it offers—the simple act of writing—will give you a tangible, accessible, and remarkably effective tool you can use to get at a task that doesn't feel simple or tangible at all.

Finally, writing is my passion, my area of expertise. It's what I have to offer the world. This book is what is trying to be expressed through *me*. And as is true with all of our unique expressions, it feels both too small and too big at the same time. This is what I have to give. So I give it humbly and without trying to decide if it is "good enough" to give.

For the past decade, I've been working with authors, helping them get their words on paper through my company. The business started as most businesses do, as a response to my own frustrations during the process of writing my first book, a story I'll detail for you in the pages that follow. It has grown over the years to be so much bigger than me. It's now a team and a community of writers just like I was, and just like you are, who know they have something to say but aren't sure how to say it just yet.

We host workshops, have a podcast, send out weekly writing prompts, and have journals and workbooks available—all aimed at helping people get unstuck in their writing so they can get unstuck in their lives. Some of these people struggle to use the term "writer" when they describe themselves. Some have no interest in writing anything that will be shared in any kind of public way. Some are experienced and successful professional authors. We help all of them find words buried inside them that are more powerful and profound than they could have found on their own—words they are shocked to discover have always been there.

We have programs like Prepare to Publish, which is aimed at helping authors get a solid book outline in place so they can get more writing done. Other programs are for writers who have no aspirations to publish a book. For example, at one of my favorite events we host every year—The Find Your Voice one-day writing workshop—we all but shock participants when we tell them to show up in clothes like workout pants or sweats. Most people think of writing as a buttoned-up activity, so participants are a bit taken aback to find a writing workshop that asks them to (for lack of a better phrase) *button down.*

Over the course of the day, we show writers—and those who swear they're not "real" writers—how moving their bodies, listening to music, considering their personal stories, and responding to some simple prompts helps them tap into insights, revelations, and wisdom they didn't know they had. All through the written word. Some attend because they have something they want to write and feel stuck. Others attend because they're stuck in some other rut—a boring job or a toxic relationship, for example—and are willing to give writing a shot as a tool to help them make a shift. All of them leave with clarity, motivation, and confidence they didn't have when they came to us.

I stumbled into this work somewhat accidentally, but what we're doing is not accidental at all. We walk participants through a proven process, backed by research, to use writing to create mental clarity, reduce anxiety, improve their confidence, strengthen their immune systems, and—wouldn't you know it—get more writing done. A handful of them do write books, but the vast majority of them do not. And whether they ever publish their words or not, they find they have quite a bit in common.

Maybe this is because there are strong parallels between the book-writing process and the process of learning to express *anything* in our lives. Things like resistance to starting, the helpfulness of a clear plan, the way the creative process is both predictable and chaotic at the same time, and how breaking the exact plan we created for ourselves is almost always necessary in order to end up at the finish line.

In the past ten years, I've seen how, in writing as well as in life, the obstacles you face as you try to accomplish your objective are not usually the real obstacles. There are usually obstacles under the obstacles—and until you solve those "under the obstacle" obstacles, you're unlikely to make any progress.

I've watched writers get stuck, circle the same block again and again a few hundred times, and eventually give up. It's not all that different from what we do when we're trying to change a habit or a pattern in our personal lives. The world is not always friendly to our attempts to make progress, just as any author with a manuscript deadline will tell you.

I hope you're seeing the parallels here. Far too many of us short-change ourselves. We underestimate our capabilities and assume someone else is better equipped. But what if that's simply not true? What if there is no one else on the planet who can express the thing that's trying to be expressed through you? What if this is your one shot, and you don't have much time left? The thing in you that wants to be expressed can *never* be expressed through anyone else.

Not only did I begin to see these similarities, but I also started to see how the writing process itself has a way of creating change for people. Then, I started to *expect* it, it was so inevitable. As I worked with an author who was struggling to communicate in a romantic partnership, for example, things would suddenly become easier. They'd suddenly have words they didn't have before, and they'd feel they were making progress. This makes sense. Putting words on paper was helping them find the words to represent how they thought and felt about the world. The connection is clear.

But what about this? I'd be working with an author to create an outline for a business book they'd always wanted to write, and they'd have a sudden epiphany—sometimes about something totally unrelated to what we were writing about. In one case, the epiphany went on to make the author millions, and he attributed that idea to the creative process we were engaged in. This person *never even wrote the book* we worked on together, and for a while, I got down on myself about that. Had I failed him?

Or was there something about the writing process that was an inexplicable initiation to something bigger? Was the act of writing a kind of magic?

Honestly, at times the changes occurring in writers didn't seem immediately favorable. One author I worked with on a book decided, after our time together, that he wasn't going to write his book at all. Not only that, but he decided to shut down his company. He told me he'd been on the wrong path the entire time, and in a sudden surge of clarity, he completely reimagined what he was doing with his life.

This wasn't the first time I had seen something like this happen, so it didn't faze me. I felt proud of him for taking such a brave leap (which, I suppose, is easy for me to say since it was not my life that was being dismantled). It wasn't until *months* later that he emailed me to say that even though he'll never write the book we outlined together, he would pay me the money all over again in exchange for the peace of mind and clarity he feels now.

Sometimes, in order to *find your voice,* you have to step into unknown territory, into deep water. Sometimes you have to totally dismantle a thing before you can figure out how it needs to be put back together.

Writing, I have learned, has a sneaky and sort of miraculous way of helping us do that.

Over the course of years, I watched these parallels unfold through the writing process, but assumed it was my own bias toward my personal passion at work here, and I tried not to read into it too much. Maybe, I thought, I just wanted everyone to love writing as much as I did.

But then I stumbled across the huge body of research about the power of the written word to have a measurable impact on our brains and bodies. The first research I found was by a man named Dr. James Pennebaker, a research professor at the University of Texas at Austin.[2] By the time I found Pennebaker's work, it was not new. He had been studying the power of words and the impact of putting them on paper since 1997. But after reading through the data, I couldn't help but wonder: *Where had this information been all my life?*

Not only was I late to the party in discovering Pennebaker's work, but I discovered his body of research was only the tip of the iceberg. I later stumbled across Michael White and David Epstein's psychotherapeutic approach, *narrative therapy*, which has been around since the 1980s and uses the power of storytelling to help people reframe their experiences. I found Dr. Joe Dispenza's work and began to understand why our brains are more powerful than even our genetics and what it takes to change them. I read *The Body Keeps the Score* by Bessel van ker Kolk, wherein he introduces the written word as one of his key paths to recovery from trauma. He details why this process helps us access buried emotions and even offers a tool called "re-scripting" that sounded strikingly similar to what I was "accidentally" doing with my clients.

I found books like *Writing Ourselves Whole* by Jen Cross, which addresses specifically the impact of the written word for victims of sexual trauma. Then I read *Writing as a Way of Healing* by Louise DeSalvo which validated the belief I had held for so long that you could write simply because you *wanted* to write—because you felt pulled to do it—even if you had no aspirations to publish. Finally, I read *Rewrite Your Life* by Jessica Lourey, which makes a strong case for why even writing fiction is a powerful path to healing and change. Until then, I had assumed that the healing power of writing came from telling our own personal stories. Now I needed to face the reality that there was something much bigger and more mysterious going on here.

There is something miraculously healing about the power of writing it down, whether what you're writing down is fact or fiction.

As I explored this extensive body of research, I encountered firm proof to corroborate the experiences I'd been having for a decade. This was actual, measurable data that confirmed the power of writing to heal your past trauma, strengthen your immune system, and help you all-around *feel* better.

Pennebaker's research shows that writing for as little as twenty minutes a day for as little as four days in a row can cause a measurable improvement in your mood.[3] You'll see me come back to this statistic a few times in this book because its implications are so important. *A measurable improvement in your mood.* In a time when we're ingesting more mood-stabilizing drugs than ever before in the history of the world, I hope we pay attention to this small piece of data.

This is not to say that writing is a cure-all or that we should all ditch our pharmaceutical drugs in favor of a regular writing practice. It *is* to say that writing—if we're open to it—can have a measurable impact on every area of our lives, including our mental and emotional health. Words are that powerful.

Speaking of health, another piece of data from Pennebaker's work which I found particularly compelling is the finding that showed participants who wrote for four consecutive days in a row, for twenty minutes at each interval, visited the doctor's office 43 percent less often for ailments like upper respiratory infections and the flu.[4] Researchers found that even months after the experiment was over, the participants' immune systems were still stronger than their control group.

Think about this for just a minute. If writing things down on paper can have this kind of impact on our physical bodies, imagine the impact it could have on our finances, our food allergies, our emotional responses, our romantic partnerships, our careers. If a regular writing practice can have this kind of impact on your *cells*, what kind of impact do you think it can have on your spirit, your soul, your emotions, your personal life, and the wider world through you?

Perhaps the healing and peace and clarity we've been craving for so long is closer than we ever dreamed.

I can teach you how to use the power of words on the page, the way so many of my clients have, to transform the way you feel about yourself, the way you experience your life, and to supercharge your impact on the world. You might think that life is simply happening around you, the world is in chaos, and you can't do anything to control it. But that isn't true. Words can be a weapon, a battle cry, a life raft of encouragement whispered into the distance—or maybe into your own heart.

Your words can help you understand *The Hang-Up*, get out of your rut, make a positive change in your life, and ultimately, find your voice. I can show you how.

CHAPTER 2

# But I'm Not a Writer

## Why everyone stands to benefit from a personal writing practice

When I travel and speak about the power of words to transform your life, I always start by asking two questions. It doesn't matter who I'm speaking to, the size of the room, or who is in it. It could be the C-Suite of a massive organization looking to increase market share or grow its revenue. It could be a room of moms and dads in the thick of parenting. It could be an auditorium full of creatives looking to feel inspired. Either way, I start by asking, "How many of you in here would consider yourself a writer?"

I usually go on by saying, "What I mean by this is how many of you would be mingling at a cocktail party and when someone turns to you to say, 'Tell me about yourself,' you'd say, perhaps among other things, "I'm a writer." No matter where I am, the response is nearly the same. Usually it's a measly five or six hands that slowly and self-consciously make their way into the air.

Immediately, I ask the second question. "Okay then, how many of you write, compose, and send at least three emails or text messages every day?" There's usually a murmur of laughter in the room as every single hand reluctantly but inevitably goes up. The point is clear. Like it or not, writing is not an optional activity in our modern lives. You *are* a writer because you write—all the time.

You write for all kinds of reasons. You write to communicate a message, to encourage a friend, to ask someone a favor, to ask a question, to deliver information, so that you don't forget something (like an item on the grocery list, for example). Maybe you write in a journal where you can fully process your thoughts or feelings about a subject, or maybe you write down your goals as a regular practice. Maybe you write down a few things you're grateful for each morning. Or maybe you have to write a "report" for work. Either way, we're all drawn to the process of writing for one reason or another.

There are a host of reasons you hesitate to act on these impulses, which I'll get to later in the chapter. But if you've ever had the impulse at all, take a minute and acknowledge yourself. Writing is an incredibly *human* instinct—and a great one at that.

Intuitively, we know writing clarifies our thinking, gets us in touch with a higher wisdom, connects us to other people, calms our nerves, and helps us make something usable from even the most horrific situations. You won't meet many people who don't have the impulse to write. We reject the identity of "writer," hide our urges to write, act like it's no big deal or that it doesn't matter. But we secretly dream of finding a way to be seen and heard and understood, even by ourselves—something which writing readily helps us do. The urge to write is almost completely universal.

I was at the service center of my car dealership the other day, and John, who's been repairing BMWs for years, told me he's been harboring a secret idea for a screenplay. Aaron, my Lyft driver, told me he used to keep journals hidden under the mattress of his bed until one day, when his mom found them and read what he had written, out loud, to his friends. Aaron hasn't written since. Go figure.

Participants who come to our Find Your Voice one-day workshops or Prepare to Publish meetups say things like, "I've had this story burning inside me for years now. I have to get it out." I recently spoke to a pastor who called because his publisher is breathing down his neck, demanding a book proposal. He's the leader of a big church, and the publisher wants to help him package some of his sermon material. But what he said to me at the end of that call got to the heart of the matter: "I know the book they want me to write, but it's not the book I need to write. I need your help."

The *need* to write. Yes. That's what I'm getting at here. Writing to publish is one thing, and it can be a great thing. But the urge to write can't always be satisfied by the act of publishing. Because writing is not *just* writing. Writing is prayer, spirituality, self-discovery, communication, therapy, connection. The invitation and impulse to write is not just an invitation and impulse to put a few words down on the page. It's an invitation to take ownership of our lives. Writing helps us gain confidence in ourselves, our ideas, and how we move through the world. The invitation to write is an invitation to *find your voice*.

Somewhere along the way, we were sold the idea that writing is only a commodity. But what if writing could also be a lifeline?

## The Evolution of the Written Word

The problem is, we have dozens of deeply embedded cultural misunderstandings about writing that make it harder than it needs to be. These misconceptions talk most of us out of the kind of writing that is likely to have an impact on our lives and in the world. They make even the most talented and trained among us write flat and uninteresting stories. They short-circuit the miracle of the writing process, period.

Let's go back several centuries and talk about how the written word came into being. I won't walk you through a long history lesson here, but for the sake of this book, keep in mind that the written word hasn't always existed. Ancient Egyptian hieroglyphs were considered the first true writing system, and coherent texts didn't appear on the scene until about 2600 BC.[1]

In lieu of writing, human beings spent a good portion of their history observing an oral tradition, which involved passing on stories, wisdom, family traditions, and tribal rituals by word of mouth. Think of the last time you spent a few hours around a campfire, telling stories for hours with your family or friends. Recall how bonded you felt to those people. How settled you were as you spoke. How much you enjoyed that time. Also recall how those stories become *legends* over time, making their way into your psyche as fact as much as myth.

This is the power words can have in our lives.

But the limitations of the spoken word are numerous. First, we have to *remember* everything that was said. With the spoken word, we don't have a way to go back and revisit it later. For centuries, spoken word axioms proved effective at transmitting necessary data from generation to generation—like how to properly clean an elk or how to use the stars to find your way home. But our brains are not limitless. At some point, they reach capacity and are not able to store anything more.

In addition to this obvious limitation, in order for the spoken word to be effective, you have to have a direct and present listener right in front of you—and, I would argue, a receptive listener at that. Have you ever tried to tell a five-year-old to go brush his teeth *and* tie his shoes? Or how about telling someone who is scrolling Instagram about what just happened to you? You might as well be talking to a cardboard box. If you don't have a captive audience the spoken word is rendered useless.

Finally, the spoken word is often misunderstood and misinterpreted. This can happen with the written word, too, but with the written word you have the benefit (as the communicator) of refining your words until they're exactly what you mean. You have the great luxury (as the reader) of combing back through the words over and over again to triple check that they said what you think it did. You don't get these advantages with the spoken word. Whatever comes out of your mouth comes out of your mouth. Even if you correct yourself, what you said first was still said.

What happens if your spoken words get twisted and misused and remembered in a way you did not mean them? What happens if the words are forgotten?

Over time, human beings began to take some of the stories they had already told thousands of times and write them down. Some of the earliest texts included ancient Egyptian religious texts, Greek and Roman literature, and the Judeo-Christian Scriptures. Then came Buddhist religious texts, Chinese religious texts, and eventually (skipping centuries) Old English texts—*Beowulf*, for example, which you may have read in a high school or college English class.

Again, my intention here isn't to subject you to a long history lesson. My intention is to help you see that the written word evolved as human consciousness evolved. As we began to put words on the page, we also began (however slowly) to understand those who are different from us, to have a reliable way to remember details, to clarify our thoughts and ideas about things by expanding our vocabulary, and to pass our cultural and religious identity to the generations that followed.

This all sounds like a good thing, right? There's only one problem. Even as the written word became more and more common, writing was still a distinctly elite activity. In order to write, you had to have access to education, money, resources, and power. This is why history books are generally slanted, conveniently leaving out whole groups of marginalized people and their perspectives. Because those people didn't *write* the history books.

Are you beginning to see how the written word gives us power?

I've heard a handful of times that city developers make decisions about how many prisons to build in the next decade based on the literacy rates of second graders. When I sought to corroborate that claim before sharing it with you, I found there were very mixed reviews on the subject. Some people swear this is categorically untrue. Others stand by it. Here's what I could verify.

According to a study done by the Annie E. Casey Foundation in 2013, students who are not reading at grade level by the end of third grade are *four times more likely* not to graduate high school.[2] An additional study done by Northwestern University in 2009 showed that students who didn't graduate high school were 63 percent more likely to be incarcerated than college graduates.[3] So whether that first piece of data I shared is true or a well-circulated rumor, you can see where the conclusion might have come from.

The reading, comprehension, and writing skills of *seven- and eight-year-olds* tell us valuable information about how future generations will contribute to society. Some of today's second graders will be constructive members of our community, able to metabolize the details of their lives in a positive way. When I say *metabolize*, what I mean is that writing offers us a powerful way to ingest what takes place in our lives—whatever that may be—to break it down into pieces, to absorb the parts that are nutritious and good for us, and to discard what doesn't serve our growth. Like a digestion process, this gives us the ability to assimilate all kinds of experiences (not just positive ones) and use them for our benefit.

I'll say more about this idea of metabolizing our lives in chapter 13, but for now what you need to know is this: an ability to metabolize will allow some kids to metabolize their particular set of life experiences in order to create new legislation, capture ideas that serve people in compelling ways, speak up in situations where their words may not be well-received, and pass on wisdom from their missions and mistakes to the next generation. They'll be able to use their experiences and their voices as powerful tools to solve complicated problems.

Others will struggle, not because they don't have something priceless to contribute, but because they don't have the mental constructs that written words bring. These mental constructs, among other things, help us lift ourselves out of our current circumstances, no matter how dire, and see them from a new perspective. Writing helps us choose a different vantage point than we've ever taken before; it helps us persuade an audience toward an action or set of actions; it affords us the ability to make a way where there wasn't a way before. Writing gives us power. Shouldn't this power be available to everyone?

Writers create *something* where there was *nothing*. Still think you aren't a "writer"? Maybe you should become one.

If this all sounds like a big stretch to you—that the written word could have an impact on issues like mental health and suicide, the opioid crisis, mass shootings, or the gap in education, consider this research a friend of mine is doing at Vanderbilt University in Nashville. According to him, early data is showing a link between the words a person uses (in this case, spoken word) and the level of depression or suicidality of that person.[4] I asked my friend what the team of researchers is watching for when they listen to their subjects speak. He said they're paying attention to intonation, volume, pacing, and even the pauses between words. But one aspect he mentioned stuck out to me more than any other. As they're evaluating a speaker's mental health and level of suicide risk, he said they are listening for *word choice*.

I asked him to explain to me what a variance in *word choice* might have to do with someone's mental or emotional state. He said the words a person chooses to describe an experience can tell you quite a bit about how they feel about it. This much might seem obvious. If you describe an event as being "the worst day of my life," it's obviously more distressing to you than if you say it was "not my favorite."

But here's where things really get interesting. The researchers are concluding, based on early data, that the fewer words a person uses to describe an event, the smaller their range for understanding and appropriately categorizing that event.

So, to oversimplify this a bit, if a participant uses the same word or phrase (i.e.: "that sucks") for two diverse circumstances (like, "my friend died" and "my pizza has olives on it"), this shows that their ability to regulate their emotions regarding those two experiences is as limited as their vocabulary. In short, the pizza problem is measured in their brain as a tragedy *equal* to losing a beloved friend.

Researchers are starting to see that these patterns show up in written words as well as spoken words.

What if writing things down could do *more* than just predict your emotional state? What if it could actually help regulate it?

Obviously, we all know that a pizza arriving with an unfavorable topping is not the same as a friend's death. But the tentative conclusion, given this in-process research, is that when we don't have a vocabulary that reflects that understanding, our brains actually don't know the difference. The words we use matter deeply. Writing helps us not only *see* the words we're already using but then *change* the words we're using so that we can in turn change our lives.

There is something about *naming our experience*—giving it the words it deserves—that helps keep us from over-inflating an experience, or from undervaluing it. The words we use help us see and honestly evaluate the problem more clearly so we can potentially find a solution. Not just any words will do, though. They have to be the right words. Have you ever had an experience when you couldn't think of the right word for a certain topic and you felt stuck until you finally figured it out? When you can finally put the *exact right words* to something you've been feeling or living through, a deep relief comes.

Mark Twain is quoted as saying, "the difference between the almost right word and the right word is . . . the difference between a lightning bug and lightning."[5] This is the invitation writing gives us—to find the exact right words.

Take a minute and think of someone or something you'd like to better understand. If you feel like you have things pretty well figured out, and you don't spend any time wrestling through the deeper questions of life—who we are and what we're doing here—then this probably won't make any sense to you. But if you find yourself confused, lost, questioning your purpose, wondering where evil comes from or why it persists, wondering if and how you might contribute to the evil of this world and if there's more for you to learn, then consider how writing things down might become your most valuable resource. Writing gives us space to work through our biggest questions.

Maybe, for now, it's just the questions you write down. No answers at all. Maybe, over time, answers begin to come. Either way, I wonder if articulating the questions with the *exact right words* might help you feel a little more settled, a little more empowered, a little more confident in who you are and why you matter. I wonder if you might come away having left some of your stress, some of your pain, on the page. I wonder if you might find a way to express what you came here to express. I wonder if this might help you find your voice.

## The Stereotype Lives On

Each time I hear career writers get defensive about our profession—as if only certain people should be "allowed" to approach this delicate and tender task of writing—I picture myself in one of my recent writing sessions. I'm sitting at my desk on day three of no shower, the remnants of white cheddar popcorn (my current obsession) crumbled all over my keyboard, one slipper on, the other having been thrown rather angrily into the corner of the room, and think, *Yes, truly. Leave this very important work to the professionals.*

We have a whole host of narratives we've spun about who is a "real" writer and who isn't one. The challenge is, depending on who you ask, the qualifications are different. For some, being a real writer means getting a certain degree from a certain university. But I know plenty of formally trained writers from prestigious universities who don't do much writing. Others say real writers are those who sell millions of copies of their books or whose words grace the bestseller lists. If that's true, why do the writers on those lists still tell me they don't feel like real writers? It's a mystery.

Still, the myths we've created about who is a real writer and who isn't one have permeated our culture, and therefore, our psyches. I mentioned earlier about asking people to consider their earliest memory about writing. You'd be shocked how many of them *swear* they don't have one, but then put their pens to the page, and suddenly, the magic of writing takes over. Out of nowhere they remember in vivid detail how Mrs. Johnson ridiculed them in front of the whole class in fourth grade for forgetting—again—where the commas go.

These same writers are the ones who tell me they can't write because they have terrible grammar. They're the ones who swore, before I put them through the exercise, that they didn't have any early memories about writing at all. That's because the memory was buried in their subconscious, and we don't often find what's in our subconscious until we write about it. We don't see the connections that set us free until we take the time to write them down.

The thing we have to remember about the narratives we make up about who is a real writer and who isn't one is that they are just that: narratives. They may have valid origins or even have served a purpose for a period of time, but just like all the narratives of our culture and our lives, they are not fixed. We *can* rewrite them.

Still, people get concerned when I suggest everyone should write. They get really worried about the idea of diluting the pool of written wisdom out there. They ask things like, "Aren't there enough bad books in the world?" They wonder, "If anyone can write, then how will we know whose words to trust?"

In 2002, writer Joseph Epstein published an article in the *New York Times* titled, "Think You Have a Book in You? Think Again," in which he argued vehemently (and a bit condescendingly) that not everyone should write a book. And if he's talking about *publishing* a book, I get where he's coming from. But if you ask me, suggesting that not everyone should *write* a book is a tragic and unjust mistake that withholds one of our most powerful tools of transformation from the very people who need it most.

Let me reiterate. There's a difference between writing and publishing. Even writers who are planning to publish have to understand this distinction—there's a divide between the art of crafting a story and the business of selling a product. The two can go hand in hand, but they require a different lens. So I'm not suggesting everyone should write a book that will sit on a bookstore shelf someday. But I liken Epstein's "bad books" logic to saying to a friend who is thinking of having a baby, "Really? I mean, aren't there enough bad humans in the world?" What a crass and unhelpful comment in the wake of someone admitting the very human and vulnerable impulse they have to create something from nothing.

And besides, to what other art form do we carry this mentality? Should I never bake a cake because I've never won any baking competitions? Should I never run a marathon because I'll never break a record or be a top finisher in my age class? Should I avoid enrolling in piano lessons because I have no shot at being a concert pianist? Or do we treat all of these things the way I'm asking us to treat writing: as a form of entertainment, a chance to learn something new about ourselves and the world, a way to connect with our friends and family, and a gateway to our own souls?

Never before has writing been such a popular path, and never before have we been so skeptical of it. The rise of social media, blogging, and self-publishing (and text messaging and email communication) has made writing an inevitability for every adult in the modern world. Still, for some strange reason, we cannot let go of this idea that "certain" people should be counted out. Overall, we are left feeling like some people might be better off never picking up the pen, and that perhaps we're one of them.

## Writing That Heals You

We often overevaluate what it means to write something. To demystify the act of putting words on paper, I want to introduce you to a term I'm going to use over and over again in the pages that follow: *expressive writing.*[6] The simplest definition I can offer is this: *Expressive writing is the act of sharing your deepest thoughts and feelings about a subject on the page*. Expressive writing can vary from prose to poetry to stream-of-consciousness to lists of feeling words to a bulleted list of thoughts on a subject. This is the type of writing that will help you heal and understand yourself in new ways.

I say this to make it clear that you don't have to write a clinical trial or a perfectly organized event brief or a five-paragraph essay or screenplay or a book manuscript in order to do what I'm teaching you to do in this book. Your daily writing, like a grocery list or a to-do list, won't even do it. What you have to do is to consider what you think and how you feel about a subject, scribble a few words down on the page, and slowly, over time, watch your perspective and your life transform.

If I know one thing to be true about the writing process, it's that no matter how much I demystify it, you will still find reasons to disqualify yourself. This is true for writers who are new to this process, and it's equally true for writers who are experienced and even commercially successful at their craft. No matter who they are or what compels them to write, all of these writers say the same few phrases to me over and over again, almost word for word.

Those phrases go like this:

1. *I'm not a real writer.*
2. *What would I write about?*
3. *Who will read this?*
4. *This is a waste of time.*
5. *I'm stuck.*

I could spend pages and pages addressing each of these five phrases individually. And I'll more than cover these topics in upcoming chapters. But for now, what I need you to know is that it's not just you who feels like a fraud when you're writing. It's not just you who is worried that what comes out when you are honest with yourself won't be palatable to everyone who reads it. It's not just you who worries that your life is boring, and you don't have anything interesting to say. Even the most gifted, talented, trained authors I work with say these same things to me.

But what if the very things you *think* disqualify you are actually the ones that qualify you? Do you feel you need an invitation to the "elite" club of writers I'm talking about? Consider this list of insecurities your initiation. Welcome to the club.

The questions we ask ourselves about our writing are not just questions about writing. They are questions about life. *Do I have something to say that matters? What makes me qualified? Do I have what it takes to get the job done? What if I spend all this time, and it ends up being a waste? What if, when all is said and done, I am disappointed by what I see on the page? What if I am not proud of what I make?*

When we lean into this connection between life and writing, we discover one of the most beautiful gifts of the writing life: *writing practice is life practice.* Where we get unstuck in our writing, we get unstuck in our lives.

Regardless of whether or not you see yourself as a writer, or whether or not you think you have a good idea, even if you never share a single word you write, writing can give you access to a strength and resolve and clarity you never thought possible but always knew existed.

Writing will help you find your voice.

## Something to Say?

If you have constantly talked yourself out of the process of writing on the basis that "not everyone is supposed to write," I'd like you to consider a question. How do we decide who "should" write and who "shouldn't"? Should Joseph Epstein himself decide? Should we put someone else in charge? Should we indicate who should write with a blue check mark next to their name on Instagram?

The truth is, there are a thousand reasons to never put your words down on paper. There is no shortage of incredibly compelling, true, and even legitimate reasons that writing is far too much trouble:

- You don't really have the time (who does?).
- You'll never get the return on your investment that you want or deserve anyway.
- You don't have a great idea to write about.
- Someone else already had the same idea and did a better job writing about it than you could.
- Writing should simply be left for the "real" writers out there—the ones for whom writing comes more easily, the ones who are gifted or trained or experienced.

In addition to all the compelling reasons to give up before you get started, there are also a whole host of compelling reasons to begin. For one thing, writing can heal your life from the inside out: body, soul, and mind.

The difference between you and the writers you admire is not that they have something worthy to say and you don't. They have the same excuses you have. They have the same objections you have. There's only one key difference between you and them: *they're* doing it.

When that happens--when people write—something magical takes place. They not only record their message, they *become* their message. When they tell the truth, they embody the truth. They rise above their personal problems and find a way to metabolize their experience for themselves and, sometimes, for a small group of readers. They're becoming the heroes of their own stories, their own wise and trusted narrators.

What I said before about there being a thousand reasons to not put your ideas on paper is only partially true. Because when you really boil down the reasons, there are only a handful—and maybe, at the end of the day, even fewer than that. The voice that's telling you not to write is the same voice that's telling you not to do any of the other beautiful, life-changing things you want to try. The excuses are not only keeping us from our best writing. They're keeping us from becoming the kind of people we want to be in the world.

The great news? We can unravel the excuses, one by one. Expressive writing will help us get there.

So are you going to write? The point is, *you* get to decide. What an amazing gift and an incredible responsibility.

Writers write. I know this sounds simple enough, but if you consider the amount of time you spend *not* writing—considering writing, dreaming about writing, avoiding writing, wishing you could write—you'll realize how important this truth is.

If you decide you'd like to do it, it's time to finally get over your excuses and give it a try. In which case, this book is for you. It can be your road map, your companion, your biggest supporter, your sideline cheerleader as you do what so few people will ever do: find your voice.

known Ally, she's been trying to convince me that —and I have to admit I'm still a bit skeptical about that. But anyone could get me to write something, it would be her! If you're skeptical that you're a writer, she can get you to write too. All you have to do is read this book.

Amy Brown, cohost of *The Bobby Bones Show* and host of the *4 Things with Amy Brown* podcast

Ally has a rare and unique gift for helping others rediscover and share vital parts of themselves through the written word. As a longtime professional in the mental wellness space, I deeply respect the time she invested in gaining such an understanding of the psychological benefits of writing. I've personally experienced her transformational process, and her strength and wisdom shine in this powerful resource.

Miles Adcox, CEO of Onsite

Ally has written the book many of us need right now. With a perfect blend of grace and practicality, she grabs your hand and leads you into what will become a life-changing and lifelong practice of writing it all down. I don't think anyone is more qualified to be your guide through this process of building a new habit and forging new paths and possibilities for your life.

Hannah Brencher, author of *Fighting Forward* and *Come Matter Here*

*The Power of Writing It Down* is a book that speaks to the heart of writing is so important for everyone and motivates us to do it. I' the pleasure of working with Ally on numerous occasions, time, I've been challenged and encouraged to stretch my and GO FOR IT! This book provides a framework for we all have a story to tell and will help you devel yours. To all writers or future writers out there: been waiting for from the guide who cares, th

Kim Gravel, entrepr

ment, in
lendar

mpossible in the modern
ieal us: because it is a task
ve write—when we give into
g at us to put some words on
d where our attention is directed
nt that we can follow from begin-
nterruptions by screaming children
well-meaning coworkers who come
office every five minutes. Just focused
earing your own inner voice.
dy convinced you that the simple act of
ol for change. Maybe I've even talked you
ut in order for you to make tangible progress,
rough a step-by-step process for actually *doing*
ou make space for it in your packed life.

The practical tips I'm about to teach you are shockingly simple. So simple, in fact, that you may find yourself doing the thing we often do when we read books wherein the action steps seem easy. We read the words, think to ourselves, *That sounds easy,* and then move on without ever actually implementing anything we've read.

If you do that, the information you read will be received by your conscious mind but *not* by your unconscious mind. And this is not enough to create lasting change. All you will have when you finish this book is another habit added to the list of life hacks you haven't been able to master. And that's the last thing you need.

If you can bring yourself to actually practice the steps I teach you in the chapters that follow, I guarantee you will see profound results. The steps are simple—so simple that anyone can complete them. But don't let yourself be tricked into thinking that they're so simple, you don't need to actually *do* them.

Take note of this danger as you keep reading.

## A Space to Write

Without space, you won't be able to write. This might sound painfully obvious, but you'd be surprised how many people intuitively think it's the other way around. "If I had something to write about," they say, "then I'd make space." Unfortunately, creative energy doesn't work this way. The words that have the power to change our brains, our lives, our families, and our world flow where there is space for them to flow.

Mary Oliver, the late prolific poet who wrote some of the most profound words of the last century, said in a rare interview that the reason she was able to write so prolifically is that she didn't own a cell phone, and she spent an inordinate amount of time in the woods.[1] Now *that's* space.

Sadly, in the modern world, which is one of the most privileged periods in all of human history, we have access to just about everything we can imagine *except* space. Take a minute and consider Oliver's words. No cell phone. An inordinate amount of time in the woods. Do you know anyone today who lives without a cell phone? And when was the last time you spent more than a few hours in the woods?

If you want enough clarity to begin to use words as a way to change your life and change the world, if you want to tap into the inner wisdom that's waiting like a deep well inside of you, if you want the clarity and the power and the stamina and the abundance that comes from writing things down, you need to make space in your physical environment, space in your interior world of thoughts and emotions, and space on your calendar. I'll walk you through each of those three steps here in this chapter.

## Making Physical Space

Take a minute wherever you're sitting, put down the book for one second, and stretch your arms out to both sides of your body as far as they will go. Once they're out as far to the sides as they will go, stretch them up and over your head, reaching and stretching your arms, your shoulders, and the sides of your body. See if you can make yourself even longer as you stretch.

How does it feel to take up some space?

For most of us, it feels a little bit awkward. If you were in a public place while you did this, even more so. If you are a woman, or a person of color, or someone else who has been indoctrinated to believe you don't deserve to take up too much space in the world, the feeling of discomfort might have been even greater. If you just read the words above but didn't actually do anything with your arms at all, you have even more resistance to taking up space in the world—and an even greater reason to make space for your writing.

Let's talk about physical space for a minute. Close your eyes and try to picture someone you would call a "writer" getting writing done. (Then open your eyes again, because if you don't, you'll have a hard time reading the rest of the chapter.) For most people, "writer" conjures up a picture of someone impeccably dressed and posed in front of a typewriter, in a room with sun streaming through the window.

Why a typewriter when we're well into the twenty-first century, and nobody legitimately writes on typewriters anymore? Who knows? It's probably something to do with our idealized version of the writing life. I can tell you from experience that writing gets done in airplanes, on the backs of cocktail napkins, in the break room at the crappy job you're working, and in the ten minutes before you pick up your kids from soccer practice.

Sure, would it be ideal to sneak away to the woods for a few days to get some writing done, or to be able to build a beautiful new office space in the pool house out back? Of course. But right now, planning a writing trip to the woods or starting a new construction project would be a big, brilliant, and impressively creative distraction from what is trying to happen.

It doesn't have to be an especially fancy place; it doesn't even have to be a "special" place; but it does need to be a place where you can feel comfortable enough to let your guard down.

What you need is a simple, quiet, familiar, nearby place where you can go and let the words come. It could be a tiny nook in your living room where the light is just right, and you can curl up in a comfortable chair. It could be a coffee shop down the street that serves great espresso and your favorite pastry. It could be in your bedroom closet, tucked back behind your clothes, the only place your kids don't think to come looking for you. Wherever it is, make it a place where you know you can find a moment of rest and peace from the world.

Perhaps, for you, this is the "space" in front of your laptop, or a beautiful journal you bought for yourself. Maybe this "space" is inside the darkness of your noise-cancelling headphones. Maybe, like me, you find it easy to write on airplanes, a beautiful excuse to be out of touch for a few hours, a little enclave in the air. It's no cabin in the woods, that's for sure. But it works for me. And that's what you want: something that works for you.

Make space for yourself. Give yourself this gift.

Creative energy fills the space we make for it. When we're scared to create, we pack our lives and our minds and our homes with a bunch of crap we don't care about. We stuff it to the gills, and we silently send out a message to the universe: *No need for creativity here.* All filled up. All taken care of. It will be challenging to create much of anything if you don't learn to make some space in your environment.

I know I said that your physical space doesn't have to be special or elaborate, but there are a few simple things you can do to make it more conducive to writing and finding your voice. The first has to do with smell.

Smell is the sense most strongly tied to memory. You've probably heard that before. This is because smell activates the olfactory system, which is tied to the part of the brain that stores unconscious thought. When you smell the same thing over and over again, you tie this smell to a particular memory and allow your brain to "go back" to that same memory over and over and over again. This is why, when I smell Tommy Hilfiger cologne, I am transported, in an instant, back to the halls of my high school, where every tall, handsome athlete waltzed to class with an unmistakable swagger.

As it relates to Tommy Hilfiger cologne, you can see why I try to avoid cosmetics sections at malls around Christmas. But you can see the power smell can provide when it comes to your writing space. If you can attach a smell—like a candle or an essential oil—to the feelings you have when you sit down to write, you could bring that smell with you anywhere you go, and when you smell it, you'll be instantly transported back to the space you made for writing, even when you aren't "feeling" like going there.

This helps to aid the process which will happen naturally anyway, where your physical space becomes your mental space.

Take a minute and consider your physical environment. Is it messy? Impeccably clean? Scattered and disorganized? Sparsely decorated? Cold and sterile? Warm? Consider how your physical space might be a reflection of your mental and emotional space.

A few years ago, I was going through a difficult divorce, and during that time, I moved out of my house and into a small apartment. I knew the place was temporary, so to be honest, I didn't do much decorating. I didn't have a lot of money to spend and had lost most of my possessions in the divorce, but still I tried to get the apartment set up and make it as functional as possible. Then, one day, my friend Lindsley stopped by for a visit.

Lindsley is a life coach and interior designer who uses some concepts from feng shui in her coaching practices. If you're not familiar with feng shui, it's a traditional Chinese concept of design that emphasizes how our environment connects to our emotional state. Needless to say, the first thing Lindsley noticed when she arrived at my door was that the apartment number was 204, which she said was symbolic of the heart (2+0+4=6, which is the number that represents the heart center in feng shui).

"You're living in a heart house!" she said as she walked in. "How perfect, since you're healing your heart."

I wasn't so sure about the whole heart house thing at the time, but the idea sounded nice, so I went with it. We sat there talking for an hour or so about how much anxiety I was experiencing, how I was having trouble sleeping, and how I hadn't gotten any writing done in months. Lindsley looked around the room.

"Think of this place like your heart for a minute," she said. "If this is your heart, how have you decorated it?"

Immediately, I saw what she was saying. The space was sparsely decorated, immaculately clean, and had mostly hard, clean lines. There were very few textured fabrics or colors other than white, grey, and blue.

"Wow," I said. "If that's not symbolic, I don't know what is."

I was on a tight budget, but I decided I was going to spend some money to make my physical space reflect the mental and emotional space I was trying to create for myself. So I took some simple instructions from Lindsley and went to Target, checked the clearance section at West Elm, and spent some time thrift shopping to find some more earthy, natural items to bring into my new space. I found some woven blankets and even bought a few colorful paintings and prints to hang on the walls.

Thanks to Lindsley's direction, I also moved some furniture around in the space to make it more comfortable and usable and to give everything a better flow. The changes weren't complicated or expensive. It was just a matter of making them.

Before I knew it, I was sleeping better, anxiety wasn't dominating my days, and I was finally getting some writing done. Our physical space reflects our mental and emotional space.

I mention this here for a couple of reasons. One, because you might be thinking to yourself, *I don't have anywhere I can let my guard down and write. There's just no space in my house. I live with too many people. It's too small. It's too messy.* If this is what you're thinking, I want you to consider how your physical space could be reflecting a sense of mental and emotional space (or lack thereof). Don't get stuck here. Instead, ask yourself, *What does it mean that I don't have anywhere in my house—even a tiny corner—that I can call my own?*

Consider the age-old wisdom of one of our most treasured writers, Virginia Woolf, who said that if a woman wants to write, she needs to have *a room of her own.*[2] Having a space to call your own is symbolic of something much more important—space to think, to dream, to reflect, to create, and to contribute a part of yourself to the world.

The other reason I bring this up is because of the power available to you when you use your *physical* space to carve new neural pathways and make new mental space, the way I did when I spent a few hundred bucks decorating that tiny apartment. Making changes to your physical space—carving out a place in your life where you can write—will bring changes into your life, before you even write a single word

## Making Space on Your Calendar

Never before in our lives have we been so busy. In the twenty-first century, *busy* is a badge of honor. It's the first thing we say to people when they ask how we've been.

"How are things?"

"Great! Busy!"

But having no space in our calendars works a lot like having no space in our physical environments. It represents how we feel about ourselves and our right to take up space in the world.

Pause for a minute, and look at your calendar. How do you feel about it? How do you feel about the things that are on it? What percentage of the things on your calendar are things you actually *want* to do and what percentage are you doing for other reasons? Maybe it's to make someone else happy—like a concert you're going to with your spouse because it's his or her favorite band. Maybe it's to check a box—like going to church or getting your teeth cleaned.

I want you to actually pull out your physical calendar system (whatever you use for scheduling) and go through a month of your time. Make a list of the things on the calendar. And if you're someone who doesn't put most of your activities on the calendar, add the things that aren't on your calendar to the list. For example, you might not put things like "go to work" on the calendar, but since you spend eight hours of your day (at least) at the office, make sure that makes the list.

Perhaps you'll add things like, "make breakfast for the family," "pack school lunches," "drop off the dry cleaning," etc. Take about ten minutes to do this, and come up with a realistic representation of how you spend your time.

A friend told me once that we can tell a person's religion by looking at their calendar. I wasn't sure what she meant by that at first. Then I completed this activity that I'm teaching you now, and I saw what I had been missing. I made my own list, I started teaching participants at Find Your Voice workshops to make lists, and I understood exactly what she meant.

Time is the resource most limited to us on this planet. Far more than financial resources, once our time is gone, it's gone. Most of us think we get eighty years at least, but a friend of my husband was diagnosed with terminal cancer at forty-three. Two months later, he was gone—just like that. Even though we all knew the diagnosis was terminal, after he passed away, the sentiment of his family and friends was all the same: *We thought he had more time*. He left behind a wife and three young girls, not to mention half a lifetime of goals and dreams. Time is limited and precious.

Why are so many of us wasting it?

What my friend meant by seeing someone's *religion* in their calendar is that when you list out all the things you do in a day, a week, a month, and a year, you start to get a good sense of what really matters to you. Not what you *think* matters to you, or what you'd like to *say* matters to you, but what truly matters to you. Who and what you are worshipping. and by worshipping, I simply mean, who and what has your allegiance.

I don't want you to hypothetically consider making this list. I want you to actually make it. I want you to get out a pen and a piece of paper and write out the things that are on your calendar this month. *Write them down.* Then, I want you to take a look at the list in front of you and answer the questions I'm going to give you below.

Before you do that, though, know that writing things down (versus just thinking about them) forces us to face the truth we've been running from for too long. The process can range from cathartic ("Finally, I don't have to pretend anymore!") to terrifying ("How could I have been so wrong all this time?"). But as a way to encourage you to step into the discomfort of this process and toward a more fulfilling life for yourself, I'll go first and tell you what happened for me when I did this exercise.

When I listed what was on my calendar, I found most of the usual suspects: coffee dates, dinner meetings, work obligations, workouts. Nothing too out of the ordinary. But when I saw them all written there in front of me, what I realized was that it was a list of things that I hoped seemed impressive to other people but didn't really reflect who I am or what I want in my life.

I started wondering what would happen if I circled all the things I was doing during a given day, week, or month that made me feel at peace, brought me joy, or made me feel alive. There wasn't much to circle.

I realized most of my calendar was built around getting people to like me, or to think highly of me, or to decide I was a good person. Put a different way, I had given my allegiance to making sure that my friends, my family, my coworkers, my boss, my acquaintances, and even my Instagram followers (yes, it's true) applauded me and thought I was great. That was uncomfortable to admit, but it wasn't until I could see it in writing, right there in front of me, that I realized the trade I was making: I was exchanging my own happiness to gain the approval of others.

Which is why I want to encourage you to complete this practice physically, on a piece of paper, using your actual calendar. Do not do this in your mind.

Something happens when you write down your time commitments, versus just volleying them back and forth in your brain. It's going to open new insights. Give you new perspective. Drop you into a different part of your brain. Writing and thinking are connected, but they are not the same. So don't just think about making a list of the events on your calendar. And don't just think about your answers to the questions below. Physically get out a pen and paper (or the notes section on your phone) and write them down.

- What do I spend most of my time doing?
- Why am I doing these things?
- What is my "religion," according to my calendar?
- When I come to the end of my life, will I feel I spent my time well?
- Where can I make space for writing?

This might seem like a heavy-handed way to start a section about finding time on your calendar, but you'll see why I started here in just a minute. Despite the fact that time is our most limited resource on this planet, and despite the fact that I meet people every day who dream of writing something, I hear the same phrase over and over and over again: *I don't have the time.*

I'm as "busy" as the next person. I am married and about

to give birth to a baby girl at the time I'm writing this. I run a successful six-figure business with a team of five. I'm regularly on airplanes, flying to this event or that event to speak, or to network with authors who need our help. But the thought strikes me that if we are spending our most precious resources on something that doesn't matter to us so we can keep our parents happy, or so our spouse doesn't have a meltdown, or so the people in our church community don't judge us, or so our Instagram followers are impressed with us, then we're tiptoeing around on the margins of this one precious life we've been given.

This, it seems, is about far more than just writing. We've barely begun, and we're starting to uncover our own resistance to change.

Making space for writing is making space for *you*. For your thoughts, your feelings, your point of view. How much room is there in your life for you to have a point of view? How much space do you allow yourself to have a feeling that might be considered inconvenient? That makes someone else feel uncomfortable? That doesn't seem to "fit" a situation? How comfortable do you feel inserting your thoughts in a group conversation? Looking at your calendar will quickly begin to reveal the answers to you.

Can you make five or ten or twenty minutes a day for your writing?

What I'm suggesting here is not drastic. If you were going to start a new gym routine, you'd need at least twenty minutes on the treadmill, plus the time it takes to put the outfit on—and let's be honest, you'd probably have to go buy a new outfit, which could take a long time and cost money. Then you'd have to drive to the gym, do the workout, drive home, and shower afterward. That's an hour of your time, three days a week minimum.

Let me assure you, you can write in your underwear just fine. You don't have to buy any fancy accessories or equipment, unless you want to. And you don't have to leave the comfort of your home. You're beginning to see how doable this is, right?

What I'm suggesting is twenty minutes per day. If you don't have that to give, try for ten. If ten seems like a stretch, go for five. If you have more than twenty minutes to give, great. You'll see even more progress, more quickly. Ease your way in. Choose just a few minutes of leisure or downtime from your day and reallocate those minutes to writing. You'll see results in line with the time you put in.

As the famous American tennis player Arthur Ashe is quoted as saying, "Start where you are. Use what you have. Do what you can."

Now I'm going to walk you through the process for actually scheduling your writing time on your calendar. It doesn't matter what scheduling tool you use—iCal, Google calendar, or a good old-fashioned day planner—I want you to add your daily writing time to your calendar.

This is another one of those places where you're likely to nod your head and think this is a great idea (or, who knows, you might think it's a crappy one) but you only perform this action in your head and not in real life. It's the danger of simplicity! It sounds so simple that you read the words and then think you've actually done it. Let me confirm for you, though: you haven't done it yet.

Grab your calendar, and walk through this with me. We're going to add writing time to your schedule.

The reason you're going to physically add your writing time to your calendar—even if it's just five minutes—is that our calendars reflect what's important to us. When we put something on the calendar, we take it seriously. Writing down a commitment makes it more real to us. Writing down *anything* makes it more real to us. Remember the last time you booked an appointment, and they told you that there was a no-show fee? You put that appointment on your calendar so you would absolutely not forget and double-book yourself.

I want you to treat this small segment of time you're carving out for yourself with the same kind of reverence and commitment that you would treat lunch with a friend at your favorite café down the street, or a doctor's appointment you make weeks in advance because it's that hard to get in, or picking up your kids from soccer practice. You would never dream of not showing up for one of those things unless you were sick or there was an emergency. So you put it on your calendar. Same with this small block of time for writing.

You're making space for yourself.

You might be wondering where on your calendar you should put this bit of time, so let me walk you through some guidelines according to the research.

Your body and brain slow down at night, before you go to bed, and then they stay in that state through the night, and into when you wake up in the morning. So two great times to schedule your writing are right when you wake up or before you go to bed.

I personally prefer morning, and when I take polls at our writing workshops, I find the ratio is about 80/20, with the winning category being those who write in the morning. But the truth is, it's different for everybody. Think about whether you're naturally a "night" person or a "morning" person. That can give you a clue. If you're still not sure, try it out. See which feels easier and more natural.

You might already be slightly anxious, thinking about how it's not possible for you to have any time to yourself in the mornings because your children are up at the crack of dawn. And maybe you're a waste of space at night, thanks to a long day at the office.

Whatever. No problem.

If you want to schedule your writing time at 10 a.m., after you get the kids off to school, or you want to schedule it at 3 p.m., when you have a lull in your work schedule, then go for it. The point of early morning and late night is to make it easier for you to "drop in" to the part of your brain where your most useful writing comes from. At those times of day, you'll have good help from Mother Nature. But that doesn't mean it won't work to write in the afternoon or late morning. Remember, "Start where you are. Use what you have. Do what you can."

Okay, so now you've taken stock of your weekly and monthly calendar, asked yourself some very existential questions about where your allegiance lies, found 5–20 minutes a day (or more) that you can dedicate to writing, and physically added those "appointments" or "reminders" to your calendar.

Tomorrow comes, you sit down to write at your scheduled time . . . Now what?

## Making Mental Space

When you have a physical place and time in which you can write, your next task is deceivingly simple.

You sit in the space you chose for your writing, at the scheduled time, with no expectation that you will write anything. Yes, you read that right. Pull out the journal and pen you love to write with, flip open your computer (make sure you take it offline) and just sit in the space, looking at the blank page. No words needed.

This might seem like an incredibly counterintuitive step in a process that's supposed to be all about finding the words and writing them down, but trust me. This is a vital part of the process (not to mention it relieves some of the pressure, right?).

You'll be shocked at what happens when you carve out some time, sit in a designated space to write, and don't actually do any writing. Suddenly, you start to see very clearly the state of your mental environment. Chances are, it's as cluttered as your physical space and calendar.

In one moment, you could literally be thinking about what four things you need from the grocery store, while also worrying about a coworker who seemed a little strange to you this morning, while also trying not to pay attention to the phone you hear buzzing in another room (*Is it mine? Who is it? What if it's my kids? What if it's an emergency?*) while also thinking about what you ate for lunch because it's giving you a little bit of indigestion. Our minds are packed with thoughts that are scattered, disconnected, contradictory, unhelpful, and impossibly loud.

Sitting down to write helps us begin the process of slowing down our thoughts with the lofty goal of being fully present—to the page, and to ourselves. To write, we have to take a deep breath, start to notice our thoughts, prioritize them, pick the one we want to focus on, follow its thread, and tune out the rest. But before we can even *begin* to write, we hear the drudgery of the inside of our minds. *I need to go to the grocery store and buy lemons and tape. Tape is a funny word. And why Scotch? Speaking of scotch, whiskey sounds nice . . .*

As you sit and don't write anything, you might notice that your thought patterns don't make much sense, that your thoughts are slightly terrifying, or that your brain feels a little blank. Some people suddenly feel worried that they have *no* thoughts (don't worry; this has never been true). Some people find themselves thinking thoughts they never in a million years expected to think. They describe it almost as if someone else is thinking for them. This is why, over the years, hundreds of writers who swore to me they weren't "real" writers, have read their journal entries to me and then exclaimed, "I don't even know who wrote that!"

Writing comes from that place—from the thoughts and feelings you didn't even know you had. The ones buried beneath your consciousness. The ones with the greatest leverage to improve your physical health, to change your habits and patterns, to break old ties, to build new neural connections and forge a new path forward.

All of this, and you haven't even written a word yet.

If you feel inspired to write down a thought or two, there's no rule against that at this point. But that's not the point. The point of this step in the process is to make space in your physical environment, on your calendar, and then just sit and see what the landscape of your interior world looks like. Maybe you draw a picture. Maybe you close your eyes and just notice. Maybe you scribble down some words. Maybe you just look at the blank page. Either way, you sit in your space, at your designated time, and pay attention.

You'll be surprised how challenging this is.

## A Word on Your Brain and Space

I don't want to bog you down with too much brain science, since I want this to be a practical and helpful tool for making more space in your life. But we're getting to the point where I can't explain to you exactly why these tactics work as well as they do—or even really help you know how to implement them—unless you understand what's happening in your brain when you make space (and when you don't).

In chapter 1, we talked about how most of your behavior on any given day is automated. That means that most of your actions, reactions, responses, and movements are *not* as carefully planned out and thought through as you might have assumed, but are programmed actions—habits that were formed to help you survive by saving you time and energy (our most valuable resource for survival).

This is why, when you break a habit or pattern that you're

used to—by going on vacation, for example—the change in pace might seem pleasurable for a bit of time. It's different and new and gives your brain some inspiring input to play with. But eventually, your brain gets tired of all the work it has to do to reimagine your whole day, and you start craving your old routine again. The brain loves the efficiency of this. So when we shake things up, even if it's a change that is good and healthy for us, the brain puts up some resistance. Suddenly, even though you've loved your vacation, you're ready to go home.

But what about when the change is more permanent? Have you ever moved to a brand-new place and find yourself feeling exhausted over the smallest things? Looking for a new grocery store, finding a dentist, trying to figure out how the recycling system works. This is because your brain has to work hard to carve all of these new pathways as it learns these new things. Eventually, it finds a way to automate all of these brand-new behaviors so you can go back to feeling like yourself again. It works in our favor that our brains automate so many things. It saves us energy. What doesn't work in our favor is that, once a behavior is automated, it becomes much harder to change.

I'll explain more about how to break these patterns using writing in a later chapter, but for now, what you need to know is that the part of our brains that holds these automated behaviors is called the *limbic brain*. This is important because the limbic brain is where all of your power for change lies, where your most creative and innovative solutions lie, and—most importantly for what we're discussing here—the part of your brain you'll need to "visit" if you're going to get much writing done. The problem is, we don't "visit" this part of our brains very often.

I like to think of the limbic brain as that old filing cabinet you keep out in the garage. It's where we store old memories that we don't need to regularly access and traumatic experiences we'd prefer not to revisit, and it's where the "systems" that run our lives are written out in detail and filed away so that we don't have to think about them. Think of this as being like the blueprint of your house that's tucked away in the attic. Just because you don't look at the blueprint very often doesn't mean it doesn't exactly mirror the structure of your house.

You can see why we don't visit the old, rusty filing cabinet very often. It seems pretty inconvenient and out of the way. Plus, we're not sure what we'll find if we go digging through it. Everything seems much more organized and orderly inside the house. So instead of venturing out to the garage, we stay inside.

The *prefrontal cortex* is sometimes called the "higher-level thinking" part of the brain, and while this is true, it's also a tad misleading. Most of our modern lives make use of the prefrontal cortex—the part of our brain that's used for carefully evaluating, planning, organizing details, time management, productivity, and efficiency. Things are organized and orderly in there. The "house" of our brains is the prefrontal cortex. It's the garage (or the basement or attic), the limbic brain, where everything is out of control.

But just because you never visit the blueprint in the attic doesn't mean it's not there. The blueprint of your house doesn't stop being the blueprint just because you rearrange the furniture. The same is true of our limbic brains. When you keep doing the same things, over and over, and you don't understand why, the limbic brain usually holds the answer.

This is why it can be so powerful to spend some time with your limbic brain—your blueprint—even though you may feel hesitant to do so.

This is also what I'm asking you to do when you make space for yourself and your writing in your life. I'm asking you to "drop out" of the part of your brain where you spend most of your days, managing details and working to be more organized and efficient. I'm asking you to get present with yourself, so you know what's really going on—in the blueprint.

Now let's talk about writing and the limbic brain. Expressive writing has a way of dropping us into the limbic brain. In fact, when writers are struggling to get writing done, I give them tactics and habits that help them turn down the prefrontal cortex for just a minute so they can get into their limbic brain and get more writing done. These habits include things that will sound familiar to you now, like using your sense of smell, creating some physical space for yourself, or writing first thing in the morning or last thing at night.

While the prefrontal cortex is indeed the "higher-level thinking" part of our brain (and we need it), what this doesn't accurately represent is that the limbic brain is much better at creativity, emotion, imagination, and play. This is the "muscle" in your brain you're exercising when you spend time in your limbic system.

When you're writing, you are going out into the garage, opening the old filing cabinet, and pulling out what is there—just to see. As you sift through the files, you're going to uncover some things that make sense to you. Like the blueprint for your current house. You might think to yourself, *This looks familiar.*

Or, it might not make a ton of sense just yet. You might write down words that feel deeply unfamiliar to you. As you follow some of the prompts I give you in this book, you may wonder to yourself, *Where on earth did* that *come from?* or *Did I really* write *that?* As you unearth a story, a dream, or an idea you didn't know you had, it's possible for it to feel like meeting a stranger, or like encountering yourself for the first time. Perhaps a bit of both.

You didn't know these were here, out in your garage all this time, but here they are: the untouched mental files that are dictating your actions, reactions, and behaviors. You've stumbled across your most powerful resource for positive change.

This is your voice.

## When Words Become Voice

People always want to know if this is a forever kind of practice. Do I still make space in my life for expressive writing? Do I do this every day, forever?

The short answer is no, of course not. I don't sit down to write every single day—the same way I don't go to the gym for a workout every single day. The point is not to have perfect attendance to your practice. The point is to have a practice, period, and to know that whenever you need it, writing is there for you.

Over time, as you get used to this, you don't have to be quite so rigid about sitting in the exact same chair, with the exact same candle burning, at the designated time you put in your calendar. Because these actions you are taking with your body will *sink into your bones*, and before you know it, taking some space in the world for what you think and feel and what matters to you doesn't feel quite so foreign. Expressing yourself doesn't seem like a distant dream.

The words that fill the space you are making will become your voice. They flow from the truest part of you, they guide you, and they help you clear out the "noise" and the clutter, so you always know how to come home. Eventually, you won't have to coax yourself to write or speak or feel or contribute. The words and the power and the flow and the change will just come.

CHAPTER 4

# The Drama of the Blank Page

## What to expect when making something out of nothing

Imagine yourself in a room surrounded by sixth, seventh, and eighth graders—mostly boys—at an inner-city school in a low-income neighborhood. None of these students speak English as a first language. In fact, there are over twenty-six languages represented in this classroom, and English literacy skills range from zero (unable to communicate in English at all) to a six or a seven (able to read or speak in English, but with low writing and comprehension skills). This is where I found myself at twenty-five years old, with nothing to support me but a master's degree and the small amount of necessary delusion that characterizes your twenties.

This was my first job after college, and I was determined to be the best at it, to change the world through my twenty-by-twenty classroom. Forget the fact that dozens of teachers before me had paved the way, building comprehensive curriculum for these students. Or that I'd been warned by my faculty, staff, and administration that this was a big task for a first-year teacher, so I should take it slow and celebrate the small victories. Forget the fact that I did not speak a second language, short of the stilted Spanish I had strung together during my three-month stay in Costa Rica a few months prior. I was determined to help these kids see how language could empower them to do anything they wanted in life. I had visions of Hilary Swank from *Freedom Writers* flashing through my head.

It was a Tuesday morning that started off like any other. Then, two twelve-year-old boys, both making their way through puberty, one taller than me and one growing a very sparse mustache, started cussing at each other and calling names during class.

Within a matter of seconds, before I could do anything about it, they were up and out of their seats, all the desks pushed to the sides of the room, and they were circling each other in the middle—*Grease* style. (Later, when I was telling the story, my brother asked, "So did they dance afterward?" They did not, in case you were wondering.)

A few other students jumped to their defense, while others looked to me to see what I was going to do. To be honest, I was frozen. I stood there, blank-faced, for several seconds. I was twenty-five years old, for heaven's sake! I had learned to write curriculum in school, not deal with hormonal teenage boys. I was not equipped for this. I imagined blood and yelling. I imagined the screaming of the other students. I mentally played out conversations with their parents. The entire movie played in my mind on fast-forward—and it was not *Freedom Writers*. I reached over to my desk for the phone.

"Send security to my room *now*!" I screamed at the push of a button.

I hung up, satisfied and waiting for the "authorities" to arrive. And as embarrassing as it is, I have to admit that the thought that went through my head at that moment was something like this: *You guys are going to be in* so much trouble *when the grown-ups get here.*

The great irony of this is, I hope, obvious. I *was* the grown-up in the room. And sure, there may have been some other adult on the way who had more experience than I did, or who had the physical stature necessary to intervene in a way that I didn't or that wasn't safe for me. But notice how quick we are, at times, to assume someone *else* has an answer that we don't have, that other people have access to wisdom that is not available to us, or that we have to wait for someone else to tell us what we can or can't do before we're allowed to act? This state of mind limits us tremendously, even when, like me in my classroom, we are the grown-ups in charge.

The reason I was afraid to own that classroom space and use my voice as the grown-up in charge is the same reason so many of us are terrified to stand up, take our seat at the table, share our hearts and our minds and our lives. It's the same reason so many of us are afraid to own the blank spaces that are already ours—our homes, our schools, our communities, our world. *We assume someone else knows better than we do.*

This is the drama of the blank page.

It's daunting to create something out of nothing, so we wait for someone else to do it.

There's a meme floating around the internet that says, "We wanted to be adults so badly . . . Now look at us." A friend reflected a similar sentiment to me recently. She said, "When I was younger, I couldn't wait to grow up so I could *finally* make my own decisions. Now I would give anything for someone to tell me what to do next." There's a certain weight and responsibility and even fear that comes with knowing we have agency. We can create whatever we'd like to create. We are grown-ups. We get to choose.

Dangit.

As parents, as teachers, as leaders in our businesses or in the world, we spend our lives trying to convince other people that this is true. We tell a friend who is stuck in a terrible relationship, "It doesn't have to be like this. You don't have to live like this!" We encourage citizens to get out there and vote because "Your voice makes a difference!" We tell our kids to "make good choices," and generally, we believe we can exert some sort of energy that would have a positive impact on our environment. But what about when it comes to us?

Have you surrendered to the reality that feels like it's been handed to you? Or do you believe that you can create and recreate your life?

As I think about that meme and what my friend said to me, I picture myself back in that classroom, frozen waiting for "the grown-ups" to show up and solve my problems. It makes me think about what makes writing so powerful and life-changing, and at the same time so terrifying and challenging: it puts us back in charge.

Far too many of us are like I was in that classroom that day: waiting for someone to show up and tell us what to do next, to answer our big questions for us, to give us a set of rules to follow that make us feel safe. We love safety and security. But innovation and creativity happen *outside* the boundaries of safety and security. The act of writing invites us to this process. It invites us to the table of creativity, to the table of our own lives.

Let's imagine that you are the CEO at the head of the table of the business of your life (because, *ahem*, you are). As the CEO—the person in charge—you have to evaluate how things are going *in every area of your life*. You can leave no stone left unturned. You must evaluate the finances. The partnerships. The work life. The parenting. The household duties. The efficiency of the "company." The satisfaction of your employees. You have to make critical choices that impact the direction of this thing.

Burying your head in the sand won't help you—and in fact, you'd be shirking your responsibility as CEO. Nobody else is going to solve your problems for you. After all, you're the CEO. Even if things are in bad shape, it's your job to help improve team morale, try something new, quit what's not working, pivot and go a different direction. You are the CEO. You're in charge.

Far too many of us are acting like "Bill," who's in the back of the boardroom getting everyone coffee, rather than like the CEO of our own lives. You might be Bill in the back of the boardroom at work, but you are not Bill in your life. You are at the head of the table! You're in charge. Writing hands you back the keys to your own life.

Still, when most of us think of picking up a pen and taking the lead once and for all, we hesitate. The reason is, we are terrified of the drama of the blank page.

## The Blank Page

When I quit my full-time job to write my first book in 2010, I had grand visions of what my writing life would look like. I pictured myself holed up in coffee shops, with the sun streaming through the windows, a hit band's album blaring through my headphones while brilliant words flowed effortlessly from my brain to my fingertips.

This was my own personal narrative of what it looked like to be a writer. And remember—these narratives are made-up.

Instead, I spent most of those early years sitting on the floor of my barely-furnished apartment, working on a personal best for "days not showered," writing copy for an erectile dysfunction ad—the only paid work I could find just before rent payment was coming up. I'd eat oatmeal for dinner again, with peanut butter, because if my calculations were correct, I could keep a meal under $1 without going to McDonald's.

Even when the paid projects I took became slightly more interesting, I found myself sitting at my desk (still sadly unshowered) with a sleeve of Girl Scout cookies close by. I told myself I could eat one after I completed each new paragraph. Bribery by cookies. This was not at all how I had pictured the writing life.

To make matters worse, I found myself in a strange and precarious position. Having left the security of a full-time job in order to "free up time" to write my book, not only did I not have a regular paycheck coming in, I was spending my days writing copy for websites or brands or brochures or eventually even other people's books. How had all my time been mysteriously taken up again? And even when I *did* have extra time, why did I darn near crawl out of my skin when I had to sit still and stare at that blank page? Here I was: finally, the master of my own schedule, as I had always hoped, and I still wasn't really writing. What was my problem?

In the decade since then, I've discovered, miraculously, that my experience was not unique. *Is* not unique. There is a certain drama involved in getting our words on the page. We'll find every reason to wriggle our way out of it. The more important the words are to our own evolution, the greater the drama. If you haven't already, read more about this particular drama in Stephen Pressfield's beautiful little manifesto, *The War of Art*.

The question then becomes: how do we make that drama matter for something?

I'd like you to consider for just a minute that no matter who you are, or how much or little you've thought about writing in your life, the drama of the blank page matters. The act of putting words on the page is a metaphor for the way we put our two feet into our lives—meaning we're no longer tiptoeing around the edges of our lives, thinking about how we wish "things" were different, but we're actually standing *inside* of our lives with all of the energy and creative power we have to bring. We make the decision to work with what we have available. And perhaps we start with not much of anything—short of some disjointed thoughts or ideas rattling around in our brains. We come with only a small offering. Over time, hopefully, we learn to turn it into something meaningful.

We create something where there was nothing.

I joked the other day that writing is one of the few tasks in which you're almost guaranteed to go backward before you go forward. You do an absurd amount of wandering in circles. You're trying to untangle an impossible knot. There are hundreds of hours of "wasted" time before you strike gold (except, ironically, those "wasted" hours are the only way to the treasure). After I made the joke, I let out a big sigh. I realized what I was saying.

It's not just writing that is this way. It's faith and relationships and parenting and building a business and everything that we do that matters in this world. So much wandering in circles. Impossible knots to untangle. Hundreds upon hundreds of "wasted" hours disciplining a child or trying to scale a business or asking yourself what you actually believe about prayer or religion or God. Will it matter for something—for anything? Will I be able to make something beautiful of this? Who knows.

The only way to find out is to get started.

Writing teaches us to do something our lives are asking us to do every day: show up. Show up to the blank page and put at least a few words on the paper, just as we show up to the story of our lives. Even if what we put on the paper are not "great" words—even if they get deleted later—they have a special way of guiding us to what is next. They are our pathway. Even if they are backward diversions, they are forward progress, since sometimes, going backward is the only way forward. Writing teaches us to make peace with the inevitable detours of a life well-lived.

Writing teaches you to be accountable for yourself, since no one can add words to your page except for you. No one can live your life in your place. As you practice, you learn you are the only one who knows what the writing should look like. You can seek advice and feedback, sure, but you are the only one who can do this—who can get your heart on the paper. You learn to use what you have, do what you can, and slowly begin to edit, rearrange, and reimagine what is possible for yourself, your family, your community, and even for the world.

You never truly know the ending when you begin. You usually do not know the ending when you begin. You sometimes think you know the ending and you discover, halfway through, that you were gravely wrong about where you were going. No matter what, you come back to the page each morning to edit, delete, retool, rework—and with just a little bit more information, resolve, and perspective than you had yesterday. You try, try, try again. Will you do me a quick favor? Go back to the beginning of this paragraph and read it again. While you do, think about this: the title of the paragraph could be, "This is about writing!" or "This is about life!" and the words would mean the same thing.

## Two Kinds of Drama

You know that friend who is always at the center of some drama? They mean well, sure. But bless their little heart (as they say in the South), there's always *something* going on with them. Always some crisis. Some desperate phone call and plea for help. Some reason they've been wronged, or taken advantage of, or victimized.

You know the one. The friend who came to mind without you needing to think about it. The one whose behavior you're trying to justify now. *They're not really* that *dramatic. They've had a hard time. They do the best they can.* Yes, that friend. That's who I want you to keep in mind during this chapter.

Do me a favor and actually think of a mugshot of a face. It's going to help you do what I'm asking you to do in this chapter, which is embrace the drama of the blank page. You have to love the drama, hate the drama, embrace the drama, and have no tolerance for the drama all at the same time. Just like you do with your friend.

I mean, you love them. But seriously? Thirteen texts at 2 a.m.?

The hard truth is that I've eased you into this process as much as I'm able, but I'm sorry to say that when you start to put words on paper, two kinds of drama are bound to surface. The first kind I'll call "outside drama," and the second I'll call "inside drama." Let's tackle the outside drama first.

I'm writing these words to you on a Friday afternoon, and they're due to my editor . . . well, today. They won't get to her today. Last week, when I sat down to write them, I got a terrifying text message from my dad telling me my sister was being rushed to the emergency room in Portland, Oregon after having a heart attack. My healthy, thirty-three-year-old, active, mother-of-three *little sister* had a *heart attack* and was headed to the emergency room. The news, of course, stopped me dead in my tracks, and even though my sister was safe and stable and in great hands within a few hours, I didn't get any writing done.

I can't blame myself.

Then, the next day came, and the plan was to catch up on all the writing I'd missed from the day before. Instead, I woke up to the news that a freak tornado had hit my old neighborhood in

Nashville, Tennessee, all but demolishing the apartment building I used to live in. I frantically texted all of my friends to make sure everyone was safe and okay. They were. Most of them were outside the tornado path altogether. Still, rather than writing, I spent the morning watching drone footage of the apartment building I used to live in, imagining myself *in* that apartment and playing out every worst-case scenario that could have happened. My writing was derailed again.

The third day came around, and now I was really behind on my writing. *But today,* I told myself, *I'm committed. Nothing is going to distract me.* Except then, my husband got word that because of the novel coronavirus—a dangerous super-virus that was spreading around the world—several cultural events were being cancelled and he was losing more than a million dollars in business. I looked around the room and reminded myself: I am safe. I have everything I need. We are not broke. Worst-case scenario, there will be a lifestyle adjustment for us. Not a big deal. Still, I could not stop playing out the worst-case scenario. My writing was completely derailed a third time.

Now, let me address something directly. Am I saying that because I decided to enter into the practice of writing, this somehow caused my sister to have a heart attack, a tornado to hit Nashville, or the coronavirus to threaten not only the health and economy of my little world, but also of the wider world at large? That would be ridiculous. What I'm saying is that when it comes to the "outside drama" of our lives, our writing has a funny way of revealing what was always there. The act of focusing our attention on a single thing (or at least attempting to do so) reveals to us how distracted we've been all along.

Forget for a minute that I had a particularly dramatic week—more than is normal for me or most people—and think about how much "outside drama" or distraction we face on a daily basis. We're bombarded every day of our lives with thousands of commercial advertising messages, we're "hooked" into the twenty-four-hour news cycle that tempts us to panic about every little thing. Our smartphones are literally designed to distract us. They're constantly dinging and ringing and alerting us, trying to get our attention.

If you are going to engage in any practice that tries to keep you present and attuned to the sound of your own inner voice—a process like *writing things down*—you are swimming upstream, culturally. Our world is not designed in a way that is conducive to this kind of attentiveness.

So when it comes to outside drama, what we need to know is that it exists, it's inevitable, and when you are staring at a blank page, entering into the process of writing, it's bound to seem much more obvious than usual. Suddenly, you'll notice how distracted the world is, and you've been living in that distraction all along.

I'll say one last thing before we move on to inside drama. *We* get to decide how we respond to outside drama—a decision that is determined by the severity of the drama, some conscious evaluation ("How much energy to I have to commit to this right now?"), and usually, quite a bit of our old programming. Pay attention to how you respond when you get a text message about a loved one who's in trouble, or a natural disaster that happens in your hometown. These things are worthy of our attention, certainly. More than worthy. But do you have the impulse, like I did, to blow past the reality of the situation and take it to worst-case-scenario level?

Do you make more of the drama than it demands?

If we're going to let outside drama pull us away from our writing, is it to do something productive to help (like fly up to Portland to take care of my three nephews, for example), or is it to panic unnecessarily about how, "She could be *dead*, and for heaven's sake, *I* could be dead if thirty-three-year-old women are having heart attacks now!" Do you see the difference? It's one thing if I walk away from my writing to go to Nashville and help clean up the rubble. It's another thing if I spend three hours of precious time watching thirty seconds of drone footage over and over and imagining a life-threatening scenario that didn't actually happen.

To be clear, I'm not beating myself up for not meeting my writing deadline. It's a writing deadline, not the end of the world. But after that week, I'm more aware than I've ever been of those old neural pathways of fear and how easy it is to sink back into them. I'm more attuned to my tendency to imagine the worst-case scenario—even though I know it's counter-productive. I understand even better how easily I become distracted and even disconnected from the life raft of my own voice, and how writing always leads me back there. This is the power of a writing practice, miraculously, even when I'm not actually writing.

## Inside Drama, Inside Job

Now that we've gotten the first kind of drama out of the way, I want to talk about the second kind of drama, *inside drama*. You might have already picked up on this, but outside drama and inside drama can be connected. Notice how the "outside drama" of the tornado and the heart attack and the virus-related event cancellations triggered my inside drama—that big, dramatic, toddler tantrum voice inside of me.

This is the voice that tells you, *Everything is falling apart* and *You should have been more prepared* and *Nobody is safe from the danger!*

It's the voice that, like your extra-dramatic friend, sends you a barrage of text messages at three in the morning over something that, at the end of it all, turns out okay. We all have this friend (outside drama), and we all have this voice living inside of us (inside drama). In fact, I would argue, part of why we keep this friend around is because of what a beautiful (and handy) distraction it is from our own inside drama. In a weird and twisted way, the outside drama feels easier to handle.

But as unrefined as inside drama is, it has so much to teach us—simply because it tells the honest, unfiltered truth. It might not be your proudest voice, but it is a voice that needs to be heard. Writing helps us do this.

What if we could learn to soothe and heal the drama inside us, so that when a real disaster hit, we'd be more present, more centered, more ready to respond with grace and care? What if the outside drama didn't feel quite so dramatic anymore?

Here's something you need to know about inside drama. Unlike outside drama, inside drama does get stirred up when we come to the blank page. Put another way: while there is no causal connection between writing and outside drama, when it comes to inside drama, the connection is undeniable.

What this means is that when you sit down to write, you can expect and predict that your inner drama queen will show up. She's part of the package deal. This is why you come here, to the blank page. So you can have a conversation with her.

You can *also* expect that part of you is not going to want to do this. This is why, when you're supposed to be writing, you'll start freaking out that you can't remember the last time you washed your sheets or cleaned out the refrigerator. I shouldn't admit this, but I have spent many a writing session cleaning crust off the condiment bottles in my refrigerator. (And it's a good thing I took care of that, too—because, I mean, imagine the consequences.)

My point is that I can almost guarantee that when you start to actually put words on paper, drama is going to surface. And when it does, I want you to think of the drama kind of like an earthquake.

I live in California, and one thing Californians are always worried about is The Big Earthquake. Rightfully so, too. We have bottles of water stored in our garage and some powdered food we can rehydrate if we need to, and we're not even a tenth as prepared as most people. I even learned recently, while listening to a survival podcast, that if The Big One hits, you're *not* supposed to run out of a building, because if you run, your legs will break.

I mean, who knew? This is important stuff, people.

Anyway, while I was writing this book, we had a few smaller earthquakes hit the LA area. They were big enough that we could feel them, but small enough that nothing fell off of any shelves or anything. No damage was done. I was telling a friend how worried this made me—that maybe these earthquakes were a sign of a bigger one coming—and how inclined I felt to really beef up our survival gear. His response surprised me.

He said it's actually a good thing that these smaller earthquakes came now. They're discharging energy, which might buy us some more time before The Big One.

I want you to think of the drama that surfaces when you look at the blank page like an earthquake discharging energy. I'm sorry to say, if it's been years or even decades since you've discharged any energy in your life, the drama might be pretty intense. The anger or grief or repressed intellect or whatever it is that's under the surface *wants* to come out, and when you give it an open door, it will do just that.

Depending on how long your repressed emotions have been down there, you might feel a bit overwhelmed by them. They might seem incredibly inconvenient or embarrassing. One client of mine, when he first opened the floodgates of expressive writing, found himself crying in a boardroom—something he'd never even done in front of his wife before. This is the drama of the blank page. But these big displays of emotion are signs of a catharsis we can trust, a catharsis that is *cleansing* us.

Here's where the earthquake analogy stops working in my favor, because unlike with an earthquake, I want to remind you that you *do* have your hand on the volume dial of your own drama. You can turn it up or down. You can decide you'd like to take it up to ten, so you can feel it all now and deal with it all now. Or, perhaps you'd like to keep the volume at two, and deal with it one chunk at a time.

This is all your prerogative. There is absolutely no right or wrong way to do it.

If you want to turn the volume up to ten, it probably means carving out *lots* of space to write, owning what comes up for you, and continuing to press into the process even when the drama comes. If you choose to do this, might I recommend that you also pull a strong support system into the process with you? Good friends. A skilled therapist. A recovery community like AA or Al-Anon. Think of it this way: if you're going to be digging into deep pain, make sure you have someone to call when the darkness tries to engulf you.

This is me, by the way—the high-volume approach. I hate doing anything halfway. I'm all in. If my hair isn't on fire, I'm not having any fun.

But if you're normal and not a total drama queen like me, then you can keep your volume at two the entire time, and it will be equally valuable. Maybe even more so. Keeping the volume at two would look like writing a few days a week. Three to four days would be ideal. Write for ten minutes at a time. Notice little bits of drama pop up. Take a break. Chew on it for a while. Go back to the page when you're ready for more.

Writing is your invitation to discharge some energy that's

been pent-up for too long. You know that feeling you get when something is eating you up, and then you vent to a friend, and you feel better? That's the power of writing it down. You get to leave your fear, frustration, stress, and anxiety on the page, and come away a little lighter.

## The Beginning of Anything

Billy Collins, the Poet Laureate in the United States for many years, and a man who understands the power of the written word, has a poem called "Aristotle" that starts like this:

> This is the beginning
> Almost anything can happen . . .[1]

He goes on to describe several beautiful images of beginnings. I won't quote the entire poem here, but you should look it up and read it for yourself. It's an unmatched description of how wonderful and terrifying it can be to *start* something—to begin. When you make the commitment to yourself that you're going to start writing down your thoughts, ideas, and feelings, and you make the space to actually do that, and then you face the drama of the blank page, you begin to realize how terrifying it is to be at the beginning of anything.

This is not how we intuitively think about new beginnings.

We would all likely say we'd love a fresh start, a clean slate, a do-over in some area of life. How amazing would it be if your life did not have to constantly be defined by that one huge mistake you made? How helpful would it be if you could take everything you know now and start your marriage all over again? How empowering would it be if you could go back to the beginning of your career and start all over again? Wouldn't you do it better the second time?

The freshness and possibility of a new beginning is the power and the symbolism of the blank page—and it's also the reason we avoid it.

New beginnings are something we hope for, and they're also something that terrifies us because they mean starting from scratch. Some of us can't even make a batch of cookies from scratch. We use that roll of dough you find in the dairy section at the grocery store. So starting from scratch when it comes to your romantic partnership or your career or as a parent feels terrifying because it *is* terrifying. This is the beginning. Almost *anything* could happen.

In this way, engaging with the blank page is a reminder that we *do* get an opportunity to start from scratch every day. In a physical sense, this might not feel true. But in a spiritual sense, it's true. Each day we start over so don't get too attached to what we did yesterday, be it good or bad. Just put some new words on the blank page.

## What the Drama Does for You

Oddly enough, drama has a way of focusing your attention. Ask someone in crisis what they had for dinner last night, and they won't remember. Like a laser, drama points us toward what needs our attention. It helps us zero in on our target.

The contradiction here is not lost on me. Drama *distracts* us but it also forces us to pay attention? Outside drama pulls us away from writing but inside drama is why we're here? To me, this is the beautiful mystery of the practice of writing, but I get that it can also be a little confusing. So if you remember nothing else from this chapter, remember this: The drama of the writing practice is not just about getting more writing done. It's about who we are becoming. Let me explain.

I got a phone call last week from a friend who's working on

his second book. This man is not only one of the most brilliant thinkers I know, he's also a strong writer. On top of that, he's a scientist who understands how the brain works, so he knows the best practices for supporting creativity. Since he has a handful of advantages when it comes to the writing process, you'd think that would make him guaranteed to navigate the whole thing without a glitch.

When he called, he had the frantic tone many authors get mid-project. It can be a bit like temporary insanity—you sort of lose touch with normal life. When you're living in book world, time spins on in your regular life. Because of the work I do, I have come to expect this, meaning I wasn't completely surprised to hear the otherwise surprising words out of his mouth.

"My deadline is coming, and I don't think I can finish. I'm *this* close to just sending it to you." The ending of the sentence was filled with implication—sending it to *me* to *finish the book for him*.

I knew he was joking, but part of me is convinced that if I had felt particularly opportunistic in that moment, I could have quoted a price of my entire year's salary to finish the book, and he would have handed it over. That's how desperate we tend to feel when we're blocked—and on deadline to boot.

Instead, I told him to do the things he knows to do already. To go spend some time with his family. To email his publisher and ask for an extension (no one has ever died from missing a publishing deadline—if that were the case, we'd have a lot of dead authors on our hands). To go for a walk or go see a movie or drive somewhere listening to music. Anything to give his brain a break. Then I told him to come back to the page later, after he rested. The answers come much easier when we aren't struggling to find them. They come when we're relaxed enough to let them come.

Writing practice is life practice.

I also told him the other thing he already knows about writer's block. That this didn't mean he wasn't qualified to write his own book. Who could be more qualified than him? This was a normal, anticipated part of the process, and if he handed the manuscript over to me, he would miss all the goodness the book had to offer. Before it had anything to offer to his readers, his book had something to offer to him, to the person penning the words.

I told him that transformation is never easy, and that that's what was happening right now: the book was transforming him. I told him I could take a look at the chapters where he was stuck, but that I'd be short-changing him if I fixed the problem for him. He knew this. I didn't need to tell him, but it's still helpful to hear the truth sometimes. I knew he had it in him to get out of his rut on his own. When he did, he'd get to own all the clarity and confidence that comes with breaking the lock. If he didn't—and he didn't have to—he'd just find himself back in the same rut later. Writing practice is life practice.

Nobody can do it for you.

My friend hung up the phone and got back to work. A few weeks later, he finished his manuscript. I haven't read it yet, so I can't tell you if it's a masterpiece (although, knowing him, it is). But I can tell you what he said to me the next time I saw him. He said, "Thank you for sending me back to myself." Now, I didn't really do that. I just sent him back to his writing. But that's what writing will do, again and again. It will call us back to ourselves.

It will make us the strongest, most resilient, most beautiful versions of ourselves—the truest "us" that's been there all along.

In a world where it's never been easier to publish, it's never been harder to write. In a world that screams, "You're not a writer," it will be the brave and resilient few who discover a way to hear their own voice through the noise. And those who do will have something far better than fame or money or a platform or a stage. They will have the most valuable thing this life has to offer, the only thing that can never be taken from them: they will know the sound of their own voice.

CHAPTER 5

# Out of the Chaos

## Why making sense of your life starts with questions, not answers

Since great writing is born from great thinking, it shouldn't surprise you that good writing always starts with good questions. We tend to write about the things that confuse us, elude us, or inspire us to think more deeply. The questions our life is asking us are almost always the questions we're asking in our writing. The beauty of this is that our writing will help us find the answers—answers which have been there all along.

The clients I work with choose to write about things like what it means for a woman to have a miscarriage, how to navigate the unbearable loss of a loved one, how to get out from under mountains of debt, what to do when the "system" of faith you learned growing up crumbles beneath your feet, what it might be like to have a conversation with God, or how to reclaim a sense of self after traumatic abuse.

I recently coached a woman who was working on a book that was just taking shape. She grew up in the Mormon church and realized during high school that she wasn't like her peers and friends, not to mention her siblings. Now, in her writing, she'll openly say she is gay and always has been, although getting to the place where she could use those words with her family and friends took decades.

I asked her a hundred questions during our day together. Questions about what it was like to come out to her conservative Mormon family, what each of her siblings are like, and how they responded. As she told her story, I realized why this book had been burning in her, why she *had* to write it. It was helping her answer the complicated questions so many of us ask about our faith, our sexuality, and our lives:

- Am I okay?
- Can I be myself?
- If I am myself, will people reject me?
- What do I do with a faith that no longer fits me?
- Can I make peace with the parts of that faith I still love?
- Can I make peace with the people in this world who will not accept me?

The reason her writing was interesting is not because she had a degree in Mormon theology (she didn't) or because her grammar was perfect (it wasn't) or because she'd experienced some fantastical thing no one else had ever experienced (she hadn't). But the reason she had been so drawn to this project, the reason her writing was compelling, was because these questions are interesting and universal. Who *isn't* asking these questions about themselves and their lives?

Great writing begins with great questions.

Another client I worked with, named Cindi, found me through her son, Brad. Brad and I worked together, teaching workshops for another organization. One day, he called to say he thought he had a new client to send my way: his mom. Cindi had been working on her book for over a decade. She'd been compelled by the story of four young black girls who had been killed in the 16th Street Baptist Church bombing in Birmingham in 1963. She'd done copious research on the subject, spending hours upon hours at the library with binders full of photocopied documents. She'd requested official city files, and spent days of her life poring over them.

Even though Cindi had no personal connection to this story, for some reason, it had absolutely overtaken her. You'd be surprised how common this is. Sometimes we can't even explain why we're asking the questions we're asking, but we know we're asking them because they keep our attention. They get us out of bed in the morning. They wake us up in the middle of the night. These questions—even though Cindi couldn't understand it quite yet—were taking her on a long and confusing journey that wasn't going to end until she felt the questions had been answered.

The story might not have been personal to her, but the questions were. We all understand how this happens.

- Can a perfectly ordinary boy perform miraculous acts to overcome darkness in the world? This is the question that invites us into the world of Harry Potter.
- What happens when human ego goes to war with Mother Nature? This is the question that pull us into the epic movie, *Titanic*.*
- Will the rightful and worthy princess get to become queen? This is the question that drives our engagement to the cultural tale of Cinderella.

------------------

* Or, if you're a fourteen-year-old girl like I was when this movie came out, can the love of a young, dreamy Leonardo DiCaprio conquer the boundaries of wealth and class?

Interesting questions make for interesting stories, interesting writing, and interesting lives. Questions hook us and drive our writing. The connection here is palpable.

## Your Brain on Questions

Let me pause for a minute here and talk about what's happening in your brain when you ask a question. Imagine a friend sends you a message right now that says, "I have a secret to tell you. Call me later today." What are you going to be thinking about nonstop until you call your friend? You're going to be asking yourself, *What is the secret?* The fact that you know there *is* a secret, but you don't know what the secret is, will nearly drive you crazy with curiosity.

There's a reason for this. Our brains are wired to ask questions and look for answers. From an evolutionary perspective, this has helped drive our behavior to support our own survival. *Where will I find food to eat today? How will I protect myself and my family? Who can I trust, and who is an enemy? Who will I marry? What career will I choose? What will retirement look like for me?* You can see how beneficial it is for us that we are constantly asking and answering questions.

Once our immediate needs for safety are met, these questions become a bit deeper. *What really matters in my life, and what can be trimmed away? Is there a divine force that's bigger than me, and if so, how should that affect my life? What am I here for, and what makes me matter? Have I achieved everything that's possible for me? Is there more to life than this?* Again, you can see that asking and answering questions really does drive us to become the most evolved, best versions of ourselves.

Questions quite literally *hook* us into a loop, like a merry-go-round, and for better or worse, we won't get off the ride until the question is answered. This works in our favor, as I've demonstrated above, but sadly, it also works to our detriment. The same question-asking tendency that keeps us alive can also, for example, send us back to a relationship that's toxic or unlivable. We keep asking the question, *How can I make him love me?* or *How can I fix this?* But of course, in a case like this, we're on a question loop that doesn't have a great answer. The answer is, *I can't.* So you ride the merry-go-round until you decide you can accept the answer you've been given.

Notice what's happening here. These loops can be so powerful, we can learn to improve our life stories the same exact way we improve our writing: by starting with better questions. The questions we ask drive the answers we get. They set us in motion on one or more of these loops.

Writing not only reveals to us the questions that we're already asking, it also gives us an opportunity to ask better ones. It does this in a myriad of ways. If we're writing something down, and we realize it's not going anywhere or that we're feeling stuck, we can think to ourselves, *Maybe I've gotten the question wrong. How can I ask a better question?* Likewise, if we're stuck in a familiar rut (not "going anywhere") in our lives, we can think to ourselves: maybe I need to ask better questions.

The reason you love *East of Eden* is because Steinbeck uses his writing to ask the question all of us are dying to answer: Is everybody redeemable? Are there "good people" and "bad people," or are we all somewhere in-between? If there are "good" and "bad" people, which am I?

Christians from all backgrounds purchased *The Shack* in record numbers, not because William Paul Young is a great writer (although he is). We were hooked into the story because he asked a question so many of us were wondering already: *Who is God, and can I rely on him (or her) to be there for me when I'm in crisis?*

The question driving one of the bestselling books of all

time—*The Five Love Languages* by Gary Chapman—is, *How do I improve my romantic relationship?* This is a question we know has captured the attention of human beings since the beginning of time. Even a TV show like *The Bachelor* or *The Bachelorette* has gained the popularity it has, not because it's particularly refined TV (it's not) or because it makes us feel better about ourselves for having watched it (it doesn't), but because it asks a question we're all interested in knowing the answer to: *Is the fairy tale real, and can it happen to me?* The shows don't do a great job of answering the question, but audiences come back year after year, by the millions, hoping to get better answers.

Do you see how gripping these questions are?

So what does this mean for you and your writing? It means a few important things. First, if you're wondering what to write about, always start with questions. Second, if you're wondering why you feel like writing about something in particular, ask yourself, *What's the question that's under the topic?*—like Cindi with those four little girls. Is the question "Who will remember those our culture wants to forget?" Is it "Who protects the weak and vulnerable?" Is it "What happens to an innocent soul when it leaves this life?" These are all interesting questions that are worthy of exploration. Knowing the questions helps you better understand what you're writing about.

And finally, if you come to the blank page, and you don't feel like you have anything to say, consider that your lack of words might actually be a lack of questions. If what you're writing seems dull and uninteresting—even to you—see if you can write some questions instead of some answers. Start with questions, and everything gets more interesting.

We made all the arrangements, and within a few weeks, Cindi was at my home in Pasadena for our scheduled time together. She showed up at my door with three huge handfuls of Michigan sunflowers and two big bags of gifts—one for me, and one for my creative director, Annie, who was assigned to the project. This had never happened before, so Annie and I were both floored by her generosity of spirit. But Cindi assured us it was actually *we* who were generous.

"I'm so grateful and honored you're going to help me carry the story of these little girls," she said. "I don't know why these little ones are in my heart, but they are, and I cannot carry them alone."

This is how ideas come to us, and this is how we know they're ours to carry. Not that those four little girls "belong" to Cindi. That's not what I mean. What I mean is, the *questions* belong to Cindi. Whatever questions are driving her to tell the story will carry her all the way to the answers she needs in order to close the loop, in order to feel like she's written the story she hoped to write and lived the life she wanted to live. The questions might make us feel like crazy people who ought to be put in straitjackets and locked away. But do not resist them or ignore them or pretend like they're not there. Because we can either answer the questions our lives want to ask, or stay stuck in the loop forever.

What we find as we follow the path of our questions is that they know exactly where to take us. We may have always had the answers, but there's something about putting *words* to the answers—about giving voice to them—that transforms the way we see the world and the way we see ourselves in it. This is how we come to see and recognize the sound of our own voice.

## How Words Give Us Power

I've worked with a lot of clients who are "powerful" in the obvious sense of the word. They have money, influence, an audience that's paying attention. But I can tell how truly powerful someone is by how bravely they enter into their own message, and you don't have to be rich or famous to do that. We may try to dance around our messages, hoping that we can transform the world without ever letting the message transform *us*. But I have learned the hard way that this is never how it works. The message always touches us first, and then we become the embodiment of our words.

Do you see why it doesn't matter if you publish your words? You *are* your words! Or, at least, you become them over time.

I once worked with a client who was a popular pastor at a megachurch in the South. For years, he'd been onstage, preaching to thousands of people about truths he believed. Then, one day, he started to wonder if he believed those words anymore. Around this time, a publisher offered him a hefty book contract. That's when he reached out to me—to see if I could help him get his thoughts on paper.

We met to outline his book, but during our day together, I started to see inconsistencies in his message. He would say one thing one minute, and then he would say something completely different the next. As we unpacked his story, it became clear to him that he couldn't write the book the publisher was asking for. Where his life experience didn't match his old way of thinking, there were holes in his outline. His life story didn't answer the questions the way his words did.

I told him what I tell every author I work with, which is that if he wanted to write this book, he was going to have to embody it first. He was going to have to *live* this book—to become it. Then, and only then, would he be able to get the words on paper. So maybe, I said, instead of writing the book the publisher was asking for, he should write *the book he wished to become*. The second task would be much, much harder. Still, he left that day and started the task of writing. He began the task of truly finding his voice.

It's been two years since I helped that pastor outline his book, and the book isn't published yet—although, as far as I know, it's mostly written. His life has changed dramatically since then. It's changed in ways that might not seem favorable to others but that, to him, are like oxygen. He is doing it. He's making a new way for himself. He's finding the power of his own words to help him fully express himself. He's finding his voice.

This process has done far more than give him a book. It's helped him grow into himself and who he wants to be in the world!

Make no mistake: to access the power of our own words, we will have to go into our deepest darkness. We have to go into the cave and slay our dragons, as the metaphor goes, so we can come out on the other side and call ourselves brave.

You can't pretend to kill the dragons. You can't fake the kind of courage it takes to face danger like that. You cannot tiptoe around the mouth of the cave and boast about your warrior's strength and resolve. That would be ridiculous. The same is true if you want to find your voice. You either really do it, or you don't do it. There is no such thing as sort of doing it.

In case you don't believe me, I want to tell you about a man I met recently who literally saved his own life by writing down his story.

I met Robert because his publicist reached out to ask if we'd be willing to host him on the *Find Your Voice* podcast. To be honest, I don't usually take inbound requests for the podcast—not because there aren't great guests who reach out to us, but because I always have a list of people I'm waiting to interview, and we usually have episodes recorded months ahead of their publication date. But Robert's story caught my attention. Once I began reading, I knew I had to interview him as soon as possible.

One of the things that stood out to me about Robert's story was the reason he sat down to write in the first place. It was a reason I hadn't heard before—and trust me, I thought I had heard *all* the reasons. He decided to write down his story as a way to say goodbye.

During our interview, Robert told me he had always been drawn to creative writing. He recalled how, as a teenager, he wrote poetry, novellas, and short stories simply for the love of writing them. This resonated with me, and I knew it would with many of the writers we work with at *Find Your Voice*. In childhood, before we're criticized for bad grammar or getting the rules of dialogue wrong, most of us loved the act of putting our stories down on paper. It was only later—once we were divided into categories of "good writer" and "bad writer," that we decided to lay down our pens.

But there's another reason we lay down our writing utensils. Even if we make it through our education without being convinced somehow that writing isn't "for us," there's often a point in early adulthood when we decide writing (unless we're talking about emails or reports) is a frivolous and self-indulgent activity. At best, it's second to the more important demands of mature adult life.

This was what happened to Robert. It wasn't a teacher who squashed his natural, human impulse to write things down. It was simply life. It was the inevitable fast pace of the modern world, the daily demands of schedule and email. It was bills and relationships and deadlines and responsibilities. As a successful entrepreneur with expectations and obligations coming at him from every direction, there came to be less and less space in Robert's life for creative writing. He wrote emails and blog posts and articles for work (and was even praised for his writing). But he lost touch with the art and the escape of writing he had once known. He learned how to be productive and efficient with his words and his life—not to waste time doing frivolous things like writing simply because he *felt* like writing.

That is, until a memory came back to him.

This memory returned in a moment of great vulnerability, as repressed memories tend to do. While things had never been better in his professional life, Robert was struggling with his mental health and with an addiction born out of buried trauma. And the appearance of this unwanted memory tipped Robert over the edge. Isn't it unsettling how quietly and unexpectedly a thing can overcome us—even when, all other things considered, we seem to be doing quite well? As the memory crystallized in his mind, Robert made a choice. He was going to end his life.

But before he left behind friends and family for good, he decided it would be helpful to explain to them why he'd made this decision. Like an elaborate suicide note, he decided he would write down the details of his life so his family and friends could make some sense out of what he had done. He told me he wrote it because he *had* to write it. He couldn't *not* write it. I hear this from many writers—and I've experienced it myself. Sometimes there's a story we *have* to write. And yet somehow, hearing it from Robert made me understand the gravity of that phrase in a whole new way.

It's terrifying to think about a writer going into the cave of their demons through the act of writing to see if they can save their own lives.

Robert wrote and wrote and wrote. Then, somehow, through the writing of his story, he began to understand it in a new way. Writing has a way of doing this to us—helping us stand outside our stories and to see them from a new perspective. And from this new vantage point, Robert surprised himself with what he felt. It was compassion. Empathy. Forgiveness. Healing. A newfound respect and honor for himself and what he had survived. Rather than wanting to take his life, Robert suddenly felt like what he wanted to do instead was to let someone in on how he had been suffering.

It was the telling of his own story that saved his life.

I know I need to be careful in telling Robert's story. Because as powerful and appropriate as it is to point out the healing power writing can bring to even the most desperate of circumstances, it's also not fair to suggest that, when it comes to an issue as impossibly complicated as mental illness and suicide, writing is some sort of cure-all. In fact, when I spoke with Robert on our podcast, he made sure to mention that writing was only *one* of the modalities that he used to find healing through his trauma. The writing opened him up to other possibilities which included, for him, meditation, therapy, community support, and real-time vulnerability with family and friends.

So let me be clear: what I'm not saying is that writing can "cure" you of whatever problem or difficulty you are currently facing. I'm not even suggestion you *need* curing. What I'm offering is that writing is often a way to bear witness to our own lives. Sometimes this makes all the difference. Sometimes it can help to light the path before us, to put us back in touch with our own power. Sometimes it can help us ask better questions and—hopefully—get better answers. It's a way we can try at least to make sense out of the chaos. It's not everything. But it's something. And for Robert, it was the something that changed everything.

Perhaps it can be that for you, too.

# CHAPTER 6

# Stories Worth Telling

## Using *The Infinity Prompt* to turn your life into stories worth telling

The research shows there are three elements your writing needs to cover in order to have the power of change: facts, thoughts, and feelings. More specifically, the facts of whatever story you're writing, your thoughts about those facts, and then your feelings about those thoughts. I'll explain more about what this means and why it works in a minute, but for now I want to show you the kind of difference you can see in your life from words that follow this pattern, versus words that veer off on some other path. To do this, let's look at the dramatic results of another study.

In 1994, Dr. Stephanie P. Spera, Eric D. Buhrfeind, and James W. Pennebaker collaborated on a study of the power of expressive writing after job loss.[1] This study focused on a group of sixty-three middle-aged men who had all been unexpectedly laid off from their jobs in the tech industry, after working for the same company for fifteen years. Pennebaker said, "This group was the most angry, hostile, unpleasant bunch I've ever worked with."[2] Clearly, they had some energy to discharge.

The men were divided into two groups. The first group was asked to write down their thoughts, emotions, and details of their job losses. How had they suffered as a result? What were they worried about? How did their spouses feel about the change in circumstances? How did that make *them* feel? How did this change their personal plans for themselves? Meanwhile, the second group was asked to write about how they used their time at work.

The results were staggering.

"Eight months after writing, 52 percent of the emotional writing groups had new jobs compared to only 20 percent of the time management participants. Individuals from the two groups went to the same number of job interviews. The difference was that the expressive writers were offered jobs."[3]

Nearly 30 percent more likely to get a job when you go to an interview? That's what I call powerful writing.

It might help to pause for a minute and talk about why the emotional writing group saw such profound results. Was it magic? Not exactly. One strong hypothesis (which is supported by the data) is that after the layoffs, these men had some pent-up animosity about their predicament. It's not hard to understand why. Think for a minute about the earthquake example I gave in chapter 4, about small earthquakes that discharge energy before a big earthquake. That energy *needs* to be discharged, or you never know when it might come out.

In a job interview, for example.

The men who had a healthy outlet for their anger (writing) were able to discharge that "energy" in a healthy way so that the negativity didn't come out in a setting where it wasn't appropriate—where, in fact, it could hurt them. That way, when they were in their job interviews, they could focus on what was in front of them instead of getting "hooked" by questions from their past. Questions like:

- Why me?
- How could this happen?
- How could they do that to me?
- What am I supposed to do now?
- How will I tell my wife?

Writing helped them close their question loops so they could move on to something new and even better.

How might something like a healthy discharge of "energy" help in your dating life? Your career? Your family relationships? How could writing help you close the loops of your past? Loops like:

- Why did he leave me?
- What could I have done differently?
- Why did this happen?
- Are people trustworthy?
- What is the point of life?

How might answering these questions allow you to move forward rather than staying stuck where you are? It's not magic, but it does produce reliable results, which can feel pretty magical when you're stuck.

Using data from studies exactly like this one, I created a simple, yet wildly effective prompt I use with all of my clients and in my own writing practice called *The Infinity Prompt*. I wanted to make sure my clients not only had the power to write words that would effect this kind of change in their personal lives—they would be 30 percent more likely to get a job, for example—but so that they never run out of things to write about. As long as you keep living, you can keep writing and using writing for your own growth. I'm going to teach you that writing prompt here.

But before I teach you *The Infinity Prompt*, I want to give you an even clearer picture of why it works as reliably and effectively as it does.

## The Cheapest Therapy Ever

If you are a mental health professional, or even if you took Intro to Psychology in college like I did, you might recognize the three elements of expressive writing. They are also elements of the Cognitive Behavioral Therapy (CBT) model, developed by Aaron T. Beck. Since then, this model has acted as the foundation for nearly all of the basic "talk therapy" we engage in.

In other words, if you were to go to a traditional therapist's office—the kind where you sit on a couch across from a therapist and talk about your life and "how that makes you feel"—you'd be guided, more or less, by the CBT model. There are, of course, variations to it, but the CBT model has provided us with a basic understanding of human behavior and how we believe it shifts.

CBT assumes that there is a natural cause-and-effect relationship between our life stories, our thoughts, and our feelings. The cause and effect go like this:

1. Things happen to us in our lives.
2. We have thoughts about those things.
3. We have feelings that stem from those thoughts.
4. Those feelings cause us to behave or act in a certain way.
5. Those behaviors lead to outcomes.

The "raw material" of our lives is made up—more or less—of these outcomes. Let's take a look at the study I shared above and run it through this model quickly. Since I don't have the men right in front of me, I'm filling in some details I can't know for sure (their thoughts and feelings) by using my imagination. Hopefully this will help you see the cause-and-effect relationship I'm talking about.

1. A man is fired from a job to which he has dedicated fifteen years of his life.
2. He thinks to himself, "How could they do this to me?"
3. He feels angry.
4. In a job interview, the man is asked "how committed" he will be to this potential new job. The man responds by saying, a bit angrily, "How committed are *you* to your employees?"
5. He doesn't get the job.

Do you see how this cause-and-effect relationship can work? The modern talk therapy model operates on the assumption that if we can get past the events of our lives to our thoughts and feelings *about* those events, we can discover why things are happening the way they are happening. Not only that, but we have far more leverage to create change in our lives.

The newest developments in brain science back this up—and take it even a step further.

Dr. Joe Dispenza, in his book *Breaking the Habit of Being Yourself*, details what is happening in the brain while the cognitive behavioral process is taking place. He shows how a triggering event takes place, and our brains immediately send out a "signal" about that event. The signal is that little messenger that goes from one brain cell to another brain cell and says, essentially, "This is what we think about the event that just took place." This happens quickly and automatically, to the point that you might not even realize it's going on.

A driver honks at you. You think, *What's your problem?*

A stranger smiles at you. You think, *How kind.* (Or perhaps, *Is he flirting?*)

Your mom's number pops up on your phone. You think, *Okay, what have I done this time?*

Dispenza goes on to say that the neuron that travels from cell to cell is just the beginning of what's happening in your brain and your body as the cognitive behavioral model unfolds. From Dispenza's perspective, what makes this such a powerful predictor of our behavior and our outcomes is that every time a neuron fires from one cell to another cell (a neural pathway), the same cocktail of chemicals is sent to your body to make you "feel" the way that thought feels. Here's an example.

A driver honks at you. You think, *What's your problem?* and your body is flooded with adrenaline or cortisol that makes you feel furious.

A stranger smiles at you. You think, *How kind.* (Or perhaps, *Is he flirting?*) and your body is flooded with oxytocin and serotonin, the happiness and bonding drugs that make you feel drawn to a person.

Your mom's number pops up on your phone. You think, *Okay, what have I done this time?* and a familiar cocktail of "shame" drugs floods your system, so you don't pick up the phone.

So that driver could have been honking at someone else, and we'd still feel that familiar rush of anger. That stranger could be a dangerous manipulator (extreme example, but go with me), and we'd be falling in *love* with them. Your mom could be calling to tell you how proud she is of you, and you'd silence your cell phone.

The biggest mistake we all make when it comes to trying to produce measurable change in our lives—and Dr. Dispenza agrees with me—is that we get focused on changing *outcomes* when the system is driven by *thoughts and feelings.* No wonder we're stuck! We cannot control every little thing that happens to us. We might get fired, or cheated on, or abandoned by a parent. We might lose a spouse or, heaven forbid, a child. We might get a brain tumor or have an unexpected heart attack. These things are out of our control. What we *can* do, though, is rethink our thoughts and our feelings about our lives. We can change the story we're telling ourselves. In doing so, we can predisposition ourselves to the memorized feeling of *joy* rather than the memorized feeling of dread.

And guess what? Shifting these things might just as well shift our outcomes, like with the job interviews. It usually does.

Okay, that's enough psychology and brain science for now. Let me take you all the way back to the point of the conversation, which is *your writing*.

The reason writing is such a powerful tool for change is because it helps us begin to see things more objectively than we've been able to see them before. Speaking doesn't always do this for us (the limits of talk therapy are now being studied in detail[4]). But when we write, we see things as if they were happening to someone else. We begin to see our thoughts for what they are: a story we are telling ourselves that is not always helpful. And we begin to see the pattern of our feelings for exactly what they represent: memorized sensations in our bodies that predictably happen again and again and again, no matter the details unfolding around us.

Writing helps us untangle these knots. Writing helps us find a path to a new way of life and a whole new set of outcomes. That is, *if* we write words that follow this pattern. If we engage in expressive writing, we begin to ask ourselves:

1. What are the facts of the story? What happened?
2. What are my thoughts about those facts? What is the story I am telling myself?

3. How did it make me feel? Where did I experience that in my body?
4. What did I *do* because I felt that way?
5. What happened next?

This is the power of expressive writing and the power of *The Infinity Prompt*. Now you're ready to learn how to use it.

## The Infinity Prompt

To make sure you know exactly what to do, I want to do more than just teach you what *The Infinity Prompt* is, I want to walk you through it the same way I would for anyone who comes to one of our Find Your Voice one-day workshops. You'll need to pick a circumstance from your life that you'd like to write about. Maybe something specific comes to mind right away. There's something you've been mulling over and need to process. Someplace where you're stuck in one of those familiar "loops."

If nothing comes to mind right away, consider an event of your life that feels "charged." By "charged," all I mean is that it has some electricity to it. You feel it in your body. This could be something as simple as getting honked at in traffic this morning, or it could be the experience of losing your dad at a young age. Big event or small event, it doesn't matter. The point is that it is an event that matters to you.

Just in case something still doesn't come to mind, I'll say this. My husband is a person who doesn't get his feathers ruffled easily. He's incredibly evenly keeled, the yin to my yang, and when I was first explaining this prompt to him, he had a hard time thinking of *any* circumstance from his life that caused him to feel something in his body. He looked at me sideways, like I was speaking a foreign language.

If this is you, there's nothing wrong with you. In fact, you bring a great strength to those of us who feel everything in our bodies and easily lose control of our emotions. Also, this activity is going to be even more deeply healing and helpful for you than it would be for someone who answers this question more easily.

If this is you, maybe put this book down and go for a walk around the block while you think. The right-left (bilateral) motion of walking helps you think and even activates your limbic brain, where old memories are stored. Don't try to force yourself to come up with something. Trust that the right circumstance will come if you give it a little space and time.

Once you have the event you'd like to write about, get out a pen and a piece of paper and answer the following questions.

1. **Facts: What are the facts of what happened?**

   "Something" took place in your life. When you write about facts, pretend you are describing it as though it's happening in front of you on a movie screen. Or, pretend you are presenting the case in a court of law. Facts are the objective details of what happened: who, what, where, and when.
2. **Story: What is the story I am telling myself about what happened?**

   We create stories based on our *thoughts* about the facts of what has happened to us. These stories stem from our *interpretation* of what happened. A great way to get to the story is to say, "What this meant to me was . . ." or "The reason I think this took place is . . ."
3. **Feelings: How do I feel about what happened and about the story I'm telling myself?**

   A great way to name a feeling is to talk about where you *feel* it in your body. When you're scared, your heart starts racing. When you're embarrassed, your face gets flushed. When you're worried, your stomach feels twisted into knots. So take a minute and go over what you've written above—the facts and the story. What do you *feel* in your body?

4. **Actions: What did I do to engage or disengage with what I felt?**

   The action in the cognitive behavioral model is the thing you do *because* you feel the thing you felt, or to *keep* from feeling it. Most of us, being the brilliant people we are, have developed elaborate defenses against feeling unpleasant emotions like anxiety, anger, or shame. "To keep from feeling this feeling in my body, the action I take is . . ." Or "When I'm really angry, usually I . . ."

5. **Result: What was the outcome of my chosen action?**

   This is what happens as a result of your actions. For example, if your action (response to shame) is to hide, the result might be that you are isolated and alone. If you feel yourself getting defensive ("But it wasn't my fault!") or resistant ("What else could I have done?"), know that you're on the right track. This is all a natural and normal part of the journey you are on.

Let me give you an example of how this prompt might work with a circumstance from your life. Let's say, for the sake of argument, that the *fact* is that you've been single for a long time—ten years.

Now, consider for a minute the *story* a person might make up because they've been single for ten years, the thought that runs through their head so quickly and easily that they probably don't even recognize it as a thought. The story might be, "Nobody wants me," or it might be, "I'm better off alone," or maybe it's, "People always leave anyway." Whatever the story is, write it down.

What is the unpleasant feeling you might feel if you were this person who has been single for ten years who keeps telling themselves, "Nobody wants me"? Maybe you'd feel loneliness, anger, or shame. Probably a whole cocktail of unpleasant emotions. If you imagine yourself as this person, right now, where do you feel these emotions in your body? Your gut? Your chest?

Now, you'll have to do some imaginative work here, but thinking of yourself as this person who has been single for ten years, who is telling yourself nobody wants you and feeling a heaviness in your chest that feels like a cinder block weighing you down, what might you *do* to avoid feeling this way? What action might you take to protect yourself (brilliantly) against feeling so sad?

No matter what your answer is to the question (for example, "drink," or "act like the life of the party," or "try to prove that I matter by investing everything into my work," or "guard myself against potential love interests so I don't get hurt,") you can see where this is going. The result you get from this action takes you *all the way back* to the facts of the situation. Single for ten years: the very thing you want to change. We sometimes get so focused on changing the outcome of our story that we don't realize the thought pattern, memorized feeling, and brilliantly self-protective behavior have become a self-fulfilling prophecy.

Before you beat yourself up for this, remember what we said about how the human brain works. This is a brilliantly designed system that has kept you and your ancestors alive for millions of years. This "rut" is called a *neural pathway*. Your brain is doing what it was designed to do. You can change it, but in order to do so, you'll have to move your focus from outcomes to thoughts and feelings. What's the gateway that gets you there? Your *words* have the power to break the pattern.

Writing in which you name the facts, thoughts, and feelings

becomes a diagnostic tool you can use any time to get at the root of what's really going on with you, see clearly the stories you've been telling yourself, unwind the complicated emotions swirling beneath the surface, and carve a brand-new path forward.

Writing will show you the stories you've made up about your life. It will show you how those narratives are just that—made up. And it will help you change the narrative so you can change the outcome. Writing helps us step outside of our stories and see them differently. It helps us reclaim our stories for ourselves again.

When we remain unaware of facts, thoughts, and feelings we stay stuck on autopilot, living the same disappointing results over and over again. But when we bring them into our awareness through a writing practice, we give ourselves the incredible gift of clarity to see what needs to change and how. This is how we access our own agency instead of falling victim to the same old unfavorable results.

Ready for some real change in your life? *The Infinity Prompt* is potent stuff. Now that you know the process, it's time to put this practice on repeat. Twenty minutes per day. Four days per week. You'll never run out of things to write about. You can shift the way you think about your life, the way you feel about the things that have happened to you, the way you respond to the world around you, and miraculously, you can even have an impact on the results.

Nothing is left standing in your way anymore.

## Three Cautions When Writing for "Therapy"

I need to address a few important cautions about writing for personal growth. Writing is therapy, for sure. It's cathartic and an incredibly effective way to metabolize the events of your life—exactly what you're doing when you go see a therapist. But if you're going to become your own therapist without any formal training, there are some immediate concerns I'd like you to hold close. Let me dig into these concerns by telling you a story.

A woman named Amy came to one of our workshops because she was feeling stuck and was ready to use writing as a tool to find some forward momentum in her life. I asked her, along with the rest of the group, to identify one area of her life where she would like to see some forward movement. Her response was, with her body.

According to Amy, she'd been yo-yo dieting for years. Amy was tall, blonde, and the kind of woman who, if you saw her walking down the street, would probably catch your eye. She also struck me as the type who was typically immaculately dressed, since even at our workshop, where we spend over half the day up and down off the floor, her hair was perfectly blow-dried, and her nails freshly manicured.

I asked Amy to tell me the facts of the situation. In other words, what was the physical, tangible thing she was trying to change? Amy collected herself before she spoke.

"I'm fat," she said. The whole room waited.

"Okay, so you're saying the facts of the situation are that you're fat?" I asked her, to make sure I understood correctly.

"Yes, that would be the fact."

I asked Amy if it would be okay if I pushed back a little bit. She agreed. I told her that, to me, the phrase "I'm fat" felt more like a thought *about* a fact than it did like a fact itself. I waited for a minute. Then, I asked Amy if I could show her why I thought this. She nodded her head, so I turned to the rest of the room.

"How many of you here would call Amy fat? Raise your hands." Of course, not a single hand in the room went up. Amy looked around the room. This is one way to determine if the "facts" of the situation that you're trying to change are actually facts, or if they're just thoughts or feelings: ask other people if they share the same interpretation of your reality.

This is the first pitfall you might run into as you use this process for your own therapy. You might mistake your thoughts or feelings for facts.

Together, Amy and I determined what the fact of the situation actually was. After asking some probing questions, I found out that Amy had recently gained ten pounds. That was the fact. The verifiable, indisputable detail.

Next we turned to the story she was telling herself. She'd written down, "It's not just the extra weight that bothers me. It's that when I look in the mirror now, I *cringe*."

Ah, *cringe*. That sounded like a feeling to me. I asked Amy what the *thought* was that made her *feel* that cringe. She looked down at her paper.

"I wrote here . . . that I am disgusted with myself," she said.

"Disgusted is actually a feeling," I said. "But that doesn't mean there isn't a thought mixed in there, too. Could the thought be something like, 'I'm disgusting'?"

A wave of familiarity and grief washed over Amy's face. This was a "thought" she'd thought about herself a thousand times, but she had never really stopped to put words to it. Putting words to our thoughts isn't always easy, but it does give us the power to change them. This was the first time Amy had realized she was thinking such a violent thought about herself all the time.

Having a hard time applying *words* to your *thoughts* is a second pitfall you might bump into. You can see how easy it is to do that from reading Amy's example. When you encounter this obstacle, know this: you are making progress. You are taking a thought that was *unconscious* and making it *conscious*.

This, by the way, is exactly what you're doing when you're

working with a gifted therapist. Later in this book, I will give you a few tips on beginning to learn how to do this for yourself.

Am I saying that you should forego therapy (or fire your therapist) in lieu of this much cheaper option called expressive writing? Not exactly. In fact, this is the third pitfall I want to warn you about. There are a handful of great reasons to *not* take a chance on trying to be your own therapist—for example, if you're dealing with mental health issues like chronic depression or anxiety, or any kind of trauma that needs to be treated by a professional. This would be like me telling you to build your own sling when you break your arm rather than going to the doctor. That would be irresponsible—for me and for you. Please don't do that.

What I am telling you is that, even if you're struggling with your mental health, you can see why expressive writing would be such a *great pairing* for your work with a mental health professional. Expressive writing, when combined with a therapeutic process, can double or even triple your efforts by helping you multiply the therapeutic process between the times you see your therapist. What if you could begin to internalize the helpful phrases, suggestions, questions and even advice of your therapist, so it's not just an external resource for you, but an internal one? Writing can help you do this. As you keep writing, I'll show you how.

By using expressive writing in tandem with therapy, I've seen clients save thousands of dollars and years of heartache by fast-tracking their progress.

No matter who you are or what brings you to the practice of expressive writing, you do not have to figure things out alone. There are no brownie points for suffering or for getting it right. Your heart and mind are worth the investment, whatever it takes. Writing can be *like* therapy, but that doesn't mean it always replaces therapy.

Please do what is right for you.

## The Magical Power of Telling the Truth

Sometimes when we're stuck, we need to hire a therapist, and other times, we simply need to tell ourselves the truth. We might avoid the truth, dance around the truth, be terrified of the truth, or like to spin the truth, but the truth has a powerful reputation for getting us out of ruts.

If you're feeling stuck, start by telling the truth. When writers want to know what I mean by this, I take them back to *The Infinity Prompt*. What are the facts of the situation? What is the story you're making up? How is this making you feel? You might find yourself getting lazy about telling the truth—saying things like, "I'm dying," or "She is so unreasonable!" What if you got more specific?

"What does unreasonable look like?" I might ask. Now they might say things like, "She won't listen to anything I'm saying." or even better, "She talked right over me." Then I push them to get even more specific. How loud was her voice? Can you recreate the dialogue between the two of you? As we participate in this unfolding of truth, they realize something unexpected but fascinating.

Trying to tell the truth about someone else is challenging and, in the end, uninteresting. The most interesting writing, the most interesting questions, the most interesting life comes when we're able to tell the truth about *ourselves*.

Who else but you could know the fascinating and often contradictory story of your life? Who else could know the truth of what it's like to be Mormon and also a lesbian? Who else could know how you've coped with your mother's drinking problem by latching onto men who drink too, so that you can stay distracted? Who else can know that you're a pastor preaching one message on Sunday and living a totally different life the rest of the week?

Only *we* can know the truths that set us free.

Years ago, after going through a heartbreaking divorce, I decided to write a book about it. The ex-husband in my life wasn't a kind man, to say the least, and he had also been secretive about his indiscretions, so the idea of writing as a way to "tell the truth" appealed to me in a somewhat selfish way at first. I had spent years hiding his secrets—as well as hiding my own true feelings about him—and now, I figured, I could finally let it all hang out.

So I did what I do, and I sat down and mapped out the story. Hundreds of instances of gaslighting and abuse. Infidelity. Questions that went unanswered. Questionable practices with money and business. All of it. And when I felt like I finally had it all nailed down, I booked myself a stay at a cabin to see if I could write it all down.

The problem was, I started putting words on paper, and I immediately knew something was wrong. The story was boring. It was annoying, actually. I sounded like a whiny teenager complaining about how mean my boyfriend was. I mean, I'll give myself some credit since I'd been through a significant trauma, but it was quickly becoming clear to me this was not a voice I wanted to claim. It wasn't powerful or compelling in the slightest.

But do you want to know my favorite part of the expressive writing process? The words we put on the page don't have to stay the same. We get to decide how they transform. We get to expose more and more *truth* as we go on.

I had to ask myself another question: *What truth am I* not *telling?*

There's a writing exercise I give to clients where you just literally list what's true right now. It can be just a simple list, and none of the "truths" have to be connected. The only requirement is that the elements on the list have to actually *be* true. The truer the better. For example:

- There are birds chirping over my head.
- There's a gentle "shush" of the ocean out my window.
- I have a heaviness in my chest I can't explain.
- The day is bright, and I can still see the moon in the sky.

This activity has a way of bringing you back into the present moment and reminding you what is true. As I coached myself through it, the list that formed in front of me made one thing glaringly obvious: I was terrified to tell the truth about myself.

If I told the truth about myself, I'd have to explain why a twenty-eight-year-old woman walked down the aisle and married a man she did not love. That was a fascinating question, despite being a painful one to answer. It was a question I didn't have the answer to just yet, but the writing drew me in. I knew even then that this truth was going to be the most powerful truth I could ever unlock.

In the eight days that followed, I finished the story of the courtship, marriage, and divorce and was beginning to answer my own question about what makes a woman marry a man she does not love. Answering that question is what has led me here, married to a man I love deeply and expecting our first child. My husband is kind and gentle and supportive and loving and everything you want a husband to be. Even better, our partnership is without the familiar cycle of drama (that old neural pathway) that used to spin on repeat for me. Writing my story changed my life from the inside out.

The truth, as terrible as it can be, has a remarkable reputation for getting us out of ruts. Truth cuts through the B.S. that's getting in the way of the real you. Truth wakes us up and helps us pay attention. We can only know the truth about others if they choose to share it with us, but that's okay. It's the truth about *us* that transforms us. And writing is the tool that helps us to finally see it.

CHAPTER 7

# Getting Stuck (and Unstuck)

## Why your brain gets stuck and strategies to help

Stanford, Kentucky is a small farming town tucked into the middle of a long stretch of cornfields. You've probably never heard of Stanford, and rightfully so. It's a one-stoplight town—a hidden gem in the middle of nowhere—perhaps Kentucky's best kept secret. There's one little restaurant in town where the locals come for eggs, bacon, and black coffee. There's a clothing store or two, a bank building, the courthouse, a handful of stunning Victorian homes, and that's about it. If you were to fly from Los Angeles to Stanford, like I did, you'd feel like you'd been transported to another planet. And in a way, you have.

I came to Kentucky for a writer's retreat. A friend of mine was hosting the week-long event, and asked if I would work with a promising group of writers to help them make progress on their books. They were all looking to publish their work and were all in different places in the process, but all were somewhere mid-book-writing-project.

One of the first people I met at the retreat that weekend was Alex. I asked Alex to tell me more about the book he was working on, and not surprisingly, instead, he started talking about his life. It's odd but predictable how this happens, even if a writer is working on fiction. Our writing is a way to express ourselves, to untangle the knots we get wrapped up in, to metabolize the details of our lives. So it's no surprise that we cannot possibly talk about our writing without also talking about our lives.

Alex told me a story about himself and his father driving down the highway. His father was pestering him about what seemed like a meaningless detail—a cousin's birthday or something. But when his father kept picking and picking and picking at this topic (when the birthday was, which cousin's it was), Alex lost it. Suddenly, years of rage toward his father came bubbling up and boiling out in one fit of anger on one occasion. Alex demanded that his dad pull over right there on the side of the highway. He climbed out of the car.

At that moment, I wasn't quite sure yet why he climbed out of the car. But I kept in mind that the thing we need to know both in writing and in life is that needing to make sense of something too soon is often what keeps us stuck. Alex didn't need to "make sense" of this yet, for me or even for himself. He was doing something that is endlessly beneficial to the writing process—recounting a story exactly the way he remembered it happening, without worrying about making sense. Alex was *getting limbic.*

As Alex recounted this story to me, you could see the energy in his eyes. His whole body shifted. Remember how we talked about "charged" stories in the last chapter? This is what we call a "charged" story, and it's a fantastic example of getting limbic. When you think of your limbic brain, think *limbs.* You know you're limbic when you feel it in your body.

Alex apologized for getting off topic. But I knew something

he would soon know as well, after our weekend together, which is that he hadn't gotten "off topic" at all. In fact, *this* is exactly where great writing comes from.

## Your Writing and Your Life

One of the main reasons people get stuck in their writing is that they forget that writing is inextricably connected to life. In other words, where you feel stuck in your writing, you're not *really* stuck in your writing. You're stuck in your *life*. When you don't know what words to put on the page, it is almost always because you don't know what to do in your life. When you aren't sure what words to use, it's almost always because there is something you want to say or do that you feel you can't say or do without facing some kind of consequence.

So no matter how you experience being "stuck" in your writing—staring at the blinking cursor, writing thousands of words that just don't do it for you, or *not* writing at all—know this: where you are stuck in your writing, you are stuck in your life. The only way to get unstuck in your writing is to get unstuck in your life. And a fabulous way to get unstuck in your life is to get writing.

But we don't like to think about writing this way. It's easier to treat writing as a low-stakes side hobby, when the reality is that writing requires us to get up-close, personal, and gut-level honest about how we are living our lives. This can be wildly healing but admittedly uncomfortable, especially when you're just starting out.

Now that you've put some words on paper and have some skin in the game, how does being stuck in your writing mirror being stuck in your life?

- What excuses do you use to avoid your writing? Are they familiar to you?

- What topics do you find yourself writing about again and again and again?
- What words and phrases do you use repeatedly in your writing?
- Are there "charged" events from your life that you refuse to put on the page?
- What might the "off-limits" topics tell you about where you're stuck?

Wherever we find ourselves resistant to write, we will find our own resistance to seeing what is actually there.

The hardest news about writing is also the best news: writing is *diagnostic*. Where you are stuck in your writing, you are stuck in your life. Also, where you liberate yourself in your writing, you liberate yourself in your life. Using the power of the written word, you name the area where you're stuck, unpack the details of the pattern that is keeping you there, and carve a new path (literally, a new neural pathway) forward.

What I was trying to do for the writers in Kentucky is the same thing I want to do for you through the pages of this book, regardless of whether or not you ever plan to publish: give you the tools you need to *get limbic* and to get unstuck in your writing and in your life.

## Thinking Too Hard

Have you ever had an experience where you wrote something that just *came out*? Maybe it was an angry email you fired off in haste. Maybe it was a journal entry you wrote in the middle of a tragedy—a page covered in your actual tears. Perhaps it had terrible grammar but was gut-wrenchingly honest. Whatever it was for you, you know what I'm talking about. There's something about capitalizing on charged emotion that makes the writing process seem easier.

You *know* what it feels like to write from that place. Something happens in your brain and in your body, and for some unknown reason, you are not concerned anymore with sounding smart or with getting the grammar perfect. You lose all sense of the consequences that might come from writing this down. You forget the old tendency to self-edit while you write, to constantly fight to rearrange a sentence. Can you think of a time when you wrote like this?

So why do we so often suffer and struggle to get the words down? One reason this happens has to do with how our brains operate.*

I got an email from a friend the other day. It said, "I'm working on a writing project, but I keep getting stuck. It's almost like the more I think about it, the more stuck I become . . ." (Side note: she told me later that she's been calling this a "writing project" rather than what it really is, which is a novel, because the word *novel* terrifies her—another example of our stigma about writing and writers!)

The crazy thing is, the answer to her problem about being stuck is embedded right there in the question. "The more I *think* about it, the more stuck I become." Is it possible that we are stuck in our writing because we are thinking about it too much?

Let's go back and think again about that time writing came easily for you. How much were you thinking about it? Were you carefully considering every word, or were you just letting the words come as they wanted to come?

Writing, of course, takes considerable thought. But there are different *ways* of thinking about a thing, and even different parts of the brain used to do each kind of thinking. What if thinking with your frontal cortex is keeping you stuck in your writing, and

* In case you're thinking, "Oh no! More brain science!" don't worry. We'll keep this brief.

thinking with your limbic brain is what will help you get more expressive writing done?

To answer this question, let's take a look at how these two different parts of your brain operate:

| LIMBIC BRAIN | FRONTAL CORTEX |
|---|---|
| Thinks in images | Thinks in words |
| Responsible for physical sensations | Responsible for logic and reason |
| Most active when we're dreaming or moving our bodies | Most active when we're sorting, evaluating, judging, or solving a problem |
| Doesn't keep track of time (loses track of time) | Concerned with productivity, efficiency, and time management |
| Good at creativity, asking questions, and play | Concerned with answers rather than questions. Skeptical of creativity and play. |
| Memorized responses | Carefully thinks through each action |
| Makes connections between disconnected images | Connects things in logical, linear order |
| Thrives on guessing (practicing) | Thrives on certainty |
| Follows one thought at a time | Juggles many thoughts at once |

Taking a look at the list above, what part of your brain seems like it's most connected to the last time you wrote without any effort?

To be sure, if you were writing a brief for work, or outlining a presentation for your company's board of directors, you'd want to make sure you loop in your frontal cortex at some point in the process—hopefully before you share what you've written. But for now, when we're talking about expressive writing and wanting to get some words on the page—it seems like the limbic brain (that unrestricted, creative, "guessing" part of your brain) might be the part that will help you make the most progress.

This isn't all that different, honestly, from the old standby "red light, green light" brainstorming activity I learned in middle school student government. If you aren't familiar with the exercise, the rules are that as long as you are in a "green light" brainstorming session, no idea is a bad idea. It would be easy in those "green light" sessions to laugh off a crazy or unrealistic addition to the conversation ("Oh, yes—let's have *the Pope* come speak at our graduation ceremony. *That's* in the budget!") But the rules didn't allow us to do this. Any idea, no matter how insane, was added to the list.

The benefit of having these "green light" sessions—where no idea was a bad idea—was that by the time you made it to the "red light" part of the process (where you inevitably have to think critically and weed out ideas that don't make practical sense) you have far more material to work with than you would otherwise. Not to mention, sometimes a crazy, unrealistic idea inspires a similar idea that is completely doable or, at the very least, worth exploring.

The same is true with our expressive writing. If we allow our limbic brain to do its part, we come up with far more material than we would have had otherwise—the way you did when you wrote that angry email that *just came.** You were limbic. Additionally, you come up with ideas you never would have considered if you weren't able to quiet your inner editor for a minute. The "green light" activity gets all the voices in the room to speak up and tell their truth. In other words, Jamie (for example), our class treasurer who is quiet and shy and rarely shares her ideas, now feels safe to pipe in with what she's been thinking—and who knows what gems of wisdom are buried in Jamie's brain.

---

* Note: after "getting limbic," it can be helpful to wait a few hours before you hit *Send*.

What "voice" could be the metaphorical "Jamie's voice" inside your brain? Is there a part of you that's afraid to speak up because you're terrified of being ridiculed for your "crazy" ideas? Is there a piece of you that is too shy to say something because it might be criticized before it's even considered? This is what the writing process and what getting limbic will do for you. It gives *all* the parts of you permission to show up on the page. In doing so, you find the very leverage you need to grow and change: your voice.

Our frontal cortex is important. It's responsible for organizing our lives, for keeping track of time, for sorting and categorizing things, for problem-solving a faster and more efficient way to do things. Without our frontal cortex, we'd be hard-pressed to make it to a meeting on time, to pay our mortgage each month, to remember to pick up our children from school, or to have the wherewithal to remember to bring a snack for them because they're always hungry after school. This, by the way, is why artists get such a bad rap for never being on time anywhere. They're always living in their limbic system!

We need our frontal cortex.

But what if you "dropped in" to your limbic system for a period of time, to see what's there and to explore the treasures it might have for you? What would happen? Perhaps you'd come up with a profound insight. Maybe you'd uncover a creative solution. Maybe all the changes you've been working so hard to make might actually come easier. The only problem is that our culture and our lives are not organized in a way that make it easy to do this.

## Getting Limbic

You know the feeling of "getting limbic" because you've been there. Depending on your age, your cultural context, and your personality, you may have had this experience less or more often than others around you, but we've all had it.

You're limbic when you lose track of time for hours. Maybe you were playing golf, or reading a book, or surfing, or in a yoga class. Maybe you were writing in a journal, or sitting next to someone you love, or in the labor and delivery room waiting to meet your baby. All distractions fade away, and all you can see is the present moment.

You're limbic when you see the movie in your head. I tell writers to "imagine what this would look like on a movie screen" because this helps them get limbic. When you're in your limbic brain, you'll see everything in more vivid detail. Writers talk about feeling "in the zone" or "in the flow" when they're limbic, and they tend to be able to feel the sensations all over their body. They might even smell something familiar. Remember, in the chapter about *The Infinity Prompt*, when I suggested that you think of a situation from your life that feels charged? I said that sometimes you'll feel chills run up your spine, or you'll get goosebumps, or you'll feel a particular part of your body respond.

This is why that happens. A charged circumstance gets you limbic. And remember, when you think limbic, think limbs.

Similarly, you'll know when you're *not* limbic, because you won't feel anything in your body at all. You'll feel everything in your brain. You'll be "thinking too much." The more you think, the more stuck you'll feel.

I recently watched my sister, who has three young kids, make dinner from a recipe on her phone. Meanwhile, her five-year-old son was screaming questions to her from the living room like, "Mom, what team does Damien Williams play for?" and her twin two-year-old boys were trying to get inside of the stove and the refrigerator, respectively. She had to pay attention to multiple things at once—the safety of her children, the recipe for dinner. She had to be hyper-aware of time—the amount of time she had before all three kids melted down because they haven't eaten, how much time the dinner would take to cook, what time her husband would be home to join them. And she also had to prioritize tasks—pulling one two-year-old away from the stove before she answered the Damien Williams question (Kansas City Chiefs, in case you were wondering). The whole thing was quite the marvel.

There are circumstances in our modern lives—you have experienced them—when our frontal cortex is absolutely necessary for survival.

So you can see why when someone like my sister (or any of us) sits down to do ten minutes of expressive writing, we might have a hard time "letting go" of the part of our brain that we're so used to exercising. To use—what?—our limbic system? What happens if we lose track of time? What if we have a thought or feeling that disrupts this carefully thought-out system that is working right now? It can feel oddly threatening at times to drop out of our frontal cortex and into our limbic system. It can feel frivolous and foreign. It can feel like a waste of time. It's also our only way forward.

I say all this to remind you that when it comes to writing or any kind of creative process, do not assume that because you get stuck, you're doing it wrong. Getting stuck doesn't mean you're failing at writing. Getting stuck means you're *doing* writing. This is what creativity and writing is: wandering out of the certainty and into the chaos so you can try to make sense of a story, or an idea, again.

Maybe you are stuck in your writing right now—and if you aren't, you will be. Either way, welcome to the club. When you get stuck while you're writing, remind yourself: *I'm not crazy. I'm not a "bad" writer. My brain is simply doing the thing that brains do when we try to get messy and creative. It's resisting.*

That said, there are a litany of practical things we can do to help reengage our limbic brains when they go silent. Get outside and go for a walk. Go in the backyard and do some yoga. Stand up next to your desk and do some jumping jacks. I worked with an author who was a celebrity fitness trainer once—she's trained the biggest celebrities in Hollywood—and she assured me with a sly grin, "People tell *all* their secrets when their heart rates are up . . . there's something about getting the blood pumping that keeps you honest." I would amend this to, there's something about moving your body that *gets* you honest.

This is the fastest way into your limbic system. This is where your best writing will come from.

## What Gets Us Moving

Why did I start this chapter by telling you about a random small town in Kentucky? Because this special place has something to teach us about getting limbic.

Every morning we were in Kentucky, we met the writers at the one café called The Bluebird. We did this because it was a way to connect with the writers before the day began, give them some instruction, and walk them through some meditation and writing prompts before setting them free to work on their projects.

It was on the second morning that I noticed something: not a single person in that café—other than *us*—was holding a cell phone. Unlike us—writers who had traveled in from big cities and busy lives where the norm is to be in our email accounts starting at 6 a.m.—not one other person in that small town felt the same pressure. Everyone sat quietly sipping their coffee and eating their bacon.

Unfortunately, in our attempts to make our lives simpler, more productive, and more efficient, we have made it infinitely more challenging to access the part of our brain that helps us to change. We've made it virtually impossible to connect to ourselves—to our intuition, that inner knowing—and to create new possibilities out of thin air. No wonder we can't get any writing done. No wonder we're stuck.

Do you know that studies show 80 percent of smartphone users check their phones within the first fifteen minutes of waking up? This survey also showed that 83 percent of millennials sleep next to their phones, and 10 percent of those users say they wake up and check their messages in the middle of the night.[1] This isn't meant to be a tirade on smartphones, which inarguably make our lives easier in many ways. It is meant to demonstrate our un-discerning *use* of smartphones, and as a result, how challenging it is for us to stay in our limbic system, for us to lean into the tension good writing comes from.

This is why Stanford, Kentucky has quite a bit to teach us. This is why the writers who joined this retreat—like Alex—went from "stuck" in their writing to the opposite of stuck. Because we walked everywhere, and because for a few days we all gave ourselves permission to put down our smartphones and be present. As a result, floods of words came for Alex and for all of us during the four days we spent together. We gave ourselves permission to be unstructured for a bit. To not know what would come of our writing. To "green light" our limbic brains and live between the questions and the answers.

## Leaving Kentucky

Modern life is no Stanford, Kentucky, that's for sure. Our endless appointments and countless notifications and constant directions and recipes and answers to questions right in the palms of our hands isn't exactly conducive to expressive writing. With all the noise around us, how do we hear the quiet whisper of our own voice?

Do we have to move to Kentucky? It's probably not the practical answer.

Our group ultimately left Kentucky, but we continued to practice "GETTING LIMBIC" as Alex affectionately called it (and he typed it out in all caps like that in our text message threads).

"We're GETTING LIMBIC," they would tell me in the thread, sending pictures of their writing setups or their yoga mats or their journals and pens. Sure, modern life makes it challenging to live in the liminal space between questions and answers. But it *is* possible to invite that into our daily lives in a reasonable way. I know because I've witnessed it. I know because I do it.

When you get limbic, you will be swimming up the cultural stream. Others may even wonder what took you so long to respond or why you're never by your phone or why you're so "serious" about your writing. But once you've tasted the freedom of space and silence and presence and voice, you never forget. This is where the magic happens. This is the good stuff. A part of you is always trying to get back to that sweet place.

CHAPTER 8

# Write Now, Edit Later

## A mantra to help you find joy in your writing *and* your life

I had a friend who used to correct me every time I speculated about a topic. We'd be at dinner with a group of friends, and someone would say something like, "I wonder why they call them pot stickers . . ." and I'd look at the one I was about to shove in my mouth and say, "I don't know . . . maybe it has something to do with cooking them in a pot?" I didn't actually know the answer. I was just guessing. This friend couldn't stand that.

The idea that I could speculate about something I didn't know for sure absolutely infuriated this person. Almost instantly, before I was even finished speaking, he would pull out his phone and find the "true" answer so he could correct me. "Actually, the original Mandarin name for pot sticker was *guotie* . . . ." and off he'd go. It reminded me of the character named Oscar in the hit show *The Office*.

"Around here, Oscar is known as 'Actually,'" explains Jim, Oscar's coworker in the show, "because he will insert himself into just about any conversation to add facts or correct grammar."[1]

This is the "editor" brain in you. It's your "actually" brain. It's your inner Oscar from *The Office*. It's that friend across the table with the iPhone at the ready, dying to correct you any time you speculate on something. I want you to think of this as the totally accurate, totally necessary, totally helpful part of your brain—for later. For now, it's just going to get in the way of the party.

The value of "write now, edit later" isn't just that you'll get more words down on paper, it's that you'll have more fun in both your writing *and* your life. You'll get to enjoy the thrill of wondering something, guessing at it, creatively spinning a thing without that know-it-all across the table who needs you to get it perfect on the first try.

## How Do I Know This Will Work?

At Find Your Voice workshops, we focus on getting people out of their heads and into their bodies—out of their frontal cortex and into their limbic brain—so they can uncover what they truly think and feel about what's happening in their lives. We do yoga. We listen to music. We learn about the brain and how it changes. We do a bunch of writing exercises. We sometimes even share a little bit of what we've written. But whether you share anything you write or not, the point is not to write something worth sharing. The point is to discover your own truth, so you have a clear plan for moving forward.

Participants leave these workshops raving about how they feel more confident than they've felt in years. Sometimes they say they feel more "in touch" with themselves or more at peace. Another common piece of feedback we receive is that they uncovered answers to big problems—answers that had always been there but to which they just hadn't been paying attention. Our favorite response is when participants say they feel more equipped to continue the process of growth and understanding and curiosity and spirituality on their own. It's science, but it feels like a miracle.

Jamie was a participant at one of these workshops.

She had recently moved across the country, uprooting herself from friends and family and the only place she'd ever called home—all for the sake of supporting her husband, Brian, in a new business venture. Jamie and Brian had been living on the East Coast for most of their lives, but he'd been offered an opportunity in entertainment. Since the opportunity seemed like one he couldn't pass up, they came to an agreement, packed their things, and moved.

Thankfully, Jamie was able to keep her job. She was approved to work remotely, which was a huge relief. Not only did she not have to start over professionally, but she was able to work more flexible hours in whatever space felt inspiring to her. All of this helped, since moving across the country is a massive change in and of itself.

All in all, Jamie was feeling pretty good about the transition. Then, about four months into their new life, Brian announced to Jamie that he thought they should see other people. Jamie was incensed. This was more than out of left field for her; it was from another *planet*. Why on earth would she have uprooted her life and moved four thousand miles for a man who didn't want to be in a committed relationship? She had no interest in seeing other people, and she made that clear to him. But since they could not reach an agreement on that front, their marriage could not go on.

So there was Jamie, new to a city that didn't yet feel like home, just beginning to make friends—half of which had been made with Brian—and now she found herself contending with a life and a relationship that didn't look anything like she had thought it would.

But Jamie is a positive person. She has a good head on her

shoulders, and she wasn't about to let a relationship ruin her life. She was going to pick herself up and make the most of the fact that she had a career she loved, friendships that were slowly growing, and lived in one of the most beautiful places in the country.

Of course, this was all before The Monday Email.

The week before, her boss was glowing with good news during their quarterly check-in. He assured her she was doing a fabulous job. Her performance was great, he said, and the company was doing better than ever. He thanked her for her commitment to the organization, her work ethic, etc., and they spent the rest of the meeting talking about all of the exciting new opportunities ahead.

Which is what made The Monday Email so confusing. According to the email, the company wasn't doing great. In fact, they were laying off a third of the staff almost immediately. More than that, those who weren't let go immediately would be laid off slowly over the course of the next few months. Jamie had about thirty days left to work, and then a small amount of severance before she'd need a new job.

Dejected and frustrated, Jamie did her best to stay positive. At least she still had her health, she told herself, and she was employable. She'd find a new job. Maybe it was even a blessing in disguise that her marriage had ended, because now she could move anywhere. Her options were open. She felt about this the way many of us feel about new beginnings, especially when they're forced like this: excited and terrified at the same time.

Then, less than a week after that terrible email, Jamie came home to a note on her door from her landlord saying that they were selling the property, and she had thirty days' notice to vacate. At this point, she had to laugh. She laughed, laughed, and laughed some more while reading the note again and again. Then came the tears. The tears wouldn't stop. Whatever ability Jamie had to "stay positive" was being tested.

When I met her, I told Jamie that she was *living* the drama of the blank page; that for reasons we did not understand, life was clearing some space for her. Now she had space on her calendar, mental and emotional space, and a complete blank canvas to work from. I told her she was living in the tension between the questions and the answers, and that this was the most exciting part of a story. She got all of that. But then what?

When we're living the drama of the blank page, how do we actually make progress and move forward?

"Here's the most frustrating part," Jamie told the group at the workshop. "I know exactly what I want. It's not complicated."

"What do you want?" I encouraged.

"I want a partner to love and to share my life with. I want work that feels fulfilling and like I'm contributing something. And I want a few great friends. That's what I want. It's not like I'm asking for a million dollars or something." She made a big, sweeping gesture with her right hand, as if to say, "I'm not asking for the world!"

We all nodded in agreement.

"The hard part," she went on, "is that I have so little control over getting any of those things. I swipe right and left on dating apps, go on bad date after bad date, apply for job after job, and I guess I'm making progress, but it's unnerving to feel like your life is happening *to* you and you don't get much of a say about what it looks like."

"I *know* writing can help me," she said. "That's why I'm here." She held up her journal. "What I've written in this journal since I've been here is the most honest I've been with myself . . . maybe ever. I'm shocked to see the words written here, in black and white. But what now? What if writing it down doesn't help me get what I want?"

I told Jamie I was glad she was there. That she was an

inspiration to me and to all of us in the room. To come to a workshop and share your story takes more courage than most people have. To keep her heart open the way she had, in spite of all she'd been through, was brave and amazing. I also told her the best and most honest thing you can hear when you're giving yourself to a process that you hope will bring positive change to your life.

"There are no guarantees," I said.

I told her that she might write about what's going on in her life, and it might still be a long time before she got the tangible things she was talking about—the husband, the job, the great friends. The data reflects that writing *will* have an impact on her life, and likely a positive one, but there's no one who can say how long this will take or promise her that things won't get more challenging before those things come. In fact, whether we're talking about the writing process *or* your life, the terrible and miraculous thing about "write now, edit later" goes like this: the draft gets really messy before it gets good. It usually gets far messier than we would like it to get.

We would prefer to skip this part. But there's no such thing as skipping the first draft. And if we want to get a first draft down, we're going to have to *write now, edit later.*

I told Jamie I couldn't sell her a "money back" guarantee that if she wrote down exactly what she wanted, she would get it in thirty days. Sad to say, writing it down doesn't work like that. Writing, like life, is full of uncertainties, full of cloudiness and confusion, full of questions for which we do not yet have answers. I can't guarantee that Jamie, if she writes about this strange and all-consuming transition that she's in, will get a job faster, or a partner faster, or that she will miraculously know where to live.

But if and when we enter into the writing process, we do it for the same reason we engage in the process of shaping our own lives. We do it because there is an invitation that can be accepted or denied. It's your choice. There are no guarantees and there are no mandates. The real question is, do you want to try and, in trying, intentionally shape your life?

If we say yes, we don't do it because we're sure we can muscle everything into place. We say yes because we're curious, and because we have the slightest bit of faith that something beautiful might unfold. It's a mystery. We do it because, when it comes to writing and our lives, what other choice do we have?

There comes a point when it matters that you edit. In writing, this looks like cleaning up the story structure and getting better with word choice and looking up those grammar rules again. In life, it looks like stepping back and asking:

- Does my life look the way I want it to?
- Do my actions match my words?
- How can I improve as a person?
- Where do I need to be more disciplined?
- What in my life needs more awareness and attention?

Editing moments, like these, are vital and can be built into our regular rhythms and routines.

But it's also important that we don't live our entire lives in a posture of editing. What a loss it would be if all we ever did was stand back and evaluate ourselves. What a tragedy if we never just surrendered and enjoyed the miracle that we already are. Let the grace be in the writing. Don't try to make it perfect. Don't try to get it right. Just let the words "come" on the page without worrying about what they are becoming.

See if you can stop thinking so hard and needing to get it *exactly* right on the first try.

My hope, for you and for Jamie, is that you can let the grace be the part where the words just come. Maybe right now you *don't* have a positive attitude about your circumstances. Can you just write what you truly think and feel on the page, and let it be okay that it's not perfect? Can you not worry about grammar or punctuation or who might read this for just a minute?

Can you let yourself exist a little? Write now, and edit later? Let yourself take up a little bit of space?

Jamie didn't leave our workshop with clear answers about what to do next or a timeline for exactly when she'd find a job or a husband. But she left our workshop with something I'd argue she needed even more: a small measure of grace. A little bit of permission to be in the first draft of this new phase of her life. To not have to have it figured out. To be creative rather than efficient. To wonder, to practice, to laugh, and to play.

Jamie learned how to be limbic. And this, I'll remind you, is exactly how we get unstuck.

## Long In, Longer Out

I want to teach you a simple breathing exercise that you can use when you experience the temptation to edit while you are writing. You'll know when you're tempted because you'll try to write a sentence, and your frontal cortex will talk you out of it. You'll write a word, and your brain will correct you. Backward and forward, like you have one foot on the gas and the other on the brake.

When this happens, there is a very simple breathing exercise that will bring you back to your words and to yourself. You don't even have to get out of your chair. It works because it slows your brain waves and gets you out of your prefrontal cortex and into your limbic system.

All you have to do in this exercise is to make your inhale long and your exhale *even longer*. It can help to close your eyes and count.

Your count will be different from someone else's count, based on your current lung capacity. But let's say, for the sake of this example, that it takes you six counts to draw your breath all the way in, from the base of your spine up to the very top of your lungs. See if you can make your exhale last seven counts. So breathe in for six counts, out for seven.

In for six. Out for seven.

In for six. Out for seven.

In for six. Out for seven.

As you repeat this, you will feel yourself getting calmer and calmer.

Let yourself have a little more exhale than inhale, a little more grace than effort, a little more words flowing than inner editor. This does not fix everything right away, but it does make the world feel a little more peaceful and grounded. It makes you a little more open-hearted and a little more clear-headed. It drops you into your limbic system, your deep creative state. *This is the beginning. Almost anything could happen.*

CHAPTER 9

# Becoming Your Own Narrator

## How writing helps you access your inner wisdom and guide your life

Imagine for a moment that you're about to be lifted above your home in a hot air balloon. While you are secured safely to the ground, you can see one set of images, colors, shapes, and sizes. You have one perspective. Then, as you lift off from the earth, your perspective begins to widen slowly. You see angles of your home, your yard, and your neighborhood that weren't available to you before. Then, as you lift higher and higher, you see the street behind your home, each of the neighbor's yards surrounding yours.

Then, you see the street *beyond* the street behind your home, and then the street beyond that. You're not crazy that you didn't see this before. It's just that you hadn't positioned yourself at an angle where these visuals were available to you. Now that you've been lifted a few hundred feet above your home, and then a few thousand, you're able to see more. You have a different view.

This is what writing does for us. It gives us another view. It allows us the capacity to see things in our life and in our story that we were unable to see before. When you begin to write down the "facts" of the situation, like you learned to do in chapter 6, you start to think twice about what those facts really are. Instead of taking something at face value, you might walk all the way around a fact—figuratively speaking—to make sure you've accurately evaluated it. You might try to lift yourself above a feeling you're having, so you can really understand it, rather than surrendering to it as you have so many thousands of times before.

You do not have to force this to happen in your writing. It's simply what happens as part of the process. When you make space; slow down enough to process; and write down facts, thoughts, and feelings, you will inevitably let loose your own hot air balloon, and you will be amazed at the new perspective you find.

This is your "narrator voice."

When I work with authors, we spend a lot of time developing what I call a "narrator voice." The "narrator voice" is the voice that comes on-screen at the beginning of a movie and introduces the characters before we get to meet them face-to-face. This is the wise voice of reason, the mysterious voice that seems to have the answers and knows how it all ends.

The characters in the story may be suffering or struggling. The characters in the story may not know the way. But the narrator knows exactly what is coming. We follow where the narrator leads us.

The narrator voice is crucial to a story—no matter what kind of story you're writing. The reader needs to know, even if the knowledge is subtle, that there is a beginning and an end to the story, and that the events we're witnessing are taking us somewhere. Even if you never plan to put your words into a book, never plan to share them beyond yourself, pay attention to what a narrator voice might offer your life: a narrator in a story helps the viewer achieve a perspective that the hero of the story *doesn't* have.

What if there was a voice that could help you know which way to turn when you needed direction? What if a part of you had the solutions to the problems that are plaguing you most right now? How comforted would you feel if a small part of you knew that no matter what happens to you, you're going to be all right?

What if I told you that you could access this part of yourself—simply by writing it down?

## What the Narrator Knows

Think of yourself for a minute as the protagonist in your own life story. Some people express some resistance to doing this. It feels self-centered to think of themselves as a protagonist (sometimes called a hero). But before you write this off as an exercise in selfishness, consider that putting yourself at the center of your own life story is actually about personal accountability, agency, and ownership of yourself and your actions.

If you're not at the center of your story, who is?

I'm not suggesting you have to be the live-action hero of some epic film. I simply mean that in the "movie" of your life, you are at the epicenter. Your actions matter the most to how the story will unfold. At the end of your life, do you want the "story" to read, "I faced some difficult challenges. I didn't always know what to do. But I did my best and overcame unbelievable odds and was lifted by a force that felt greater than me"? Or, do you want the story to read, "It was nothing but devastation and despair and I became so overwhelmed I pretty much checked out and watched TV"?

*This* is what the narrator of the story gets to decide.

The narrator doesn't change any of the facts of the story. The narrator *frames* the story. He or she decides what the facts mean, and in doing so, gives the story a destination.

So imagine that you're the protagonist of the story you're living in, and you are trying to make a decision about what to do next, but you have no idea which way is the right way. Who *does* know the right way? The narrator. Accessing your narrator voice helps you float above your house for a minute like you did in that hot air balloon. Writing down the elements of your life as if they are a story—and thinking of yourself as the hero of that story—gives you greater perspective.

A narrator can notice things that a protagonist cannot. They can notice patterns—the facts, thoughts, and feelings that repeat again and again and again. The words that show up on your page 17,000 times when you're talking about a certain topic.

Julie, one of our workshop participants, noticed a name from her past come up in almost every single thing she wrote for months. This person, as much as she despised them, was occupying tons of space in the "story" of her life. She told me, "If I see myself write that name one more time, I am going to poke my own eyeball out." She knew it was time to deal with this individual and their power, which still held sway over her life. She never would have known any of this without the practice of writing it down.

This is the power of the narrator voice. When you begin to "narrate" your life, you're able to see things you couldn't see before, if only because you now have perspective.

## The False Narrator

The problem is that there are all kinds of voices that "narrate" our lives that are not the voice of our true narrator. This is dangerous, because the narrator drives the story. The narrator is the one who says, "She knew that job wasn't right for her, but she took it anyway. I guess she would have to learn the hard way what happens when you go against your own inner knowing."

Most of us never think of telling our stories in the third person like this, but something powerful happens when we do. We realize the answers we were searching for so hard "out there" were in our hearts and minds all along. The words that change our path almost always come from inside us.

When it comes to false narrators, I'm afraid to say most of us have dozens of them. You have what your parents say about you, what your siblings say about you and your choices, the way your best friend would narrate your life, the way your pastor or spiritual leader would narrate for you. Hopefully you have a gifted therapist who has learned to stay quiet and make space so you can finally hear your own inner voice, but if not, you even have your therapist's voice to contend with. And these are only the voices *outside* of you.

On top of all the external voices, you have the peanut gallery in your head that starts chattering away at pretty much every move you make. One therapist I worked with years ago, Chelsea Wakefield, calls this your *inner committee*—the sea of voices who weigh in on your life even when you do not ask them to. She had me name these inner voices for myself. I gave them names like "Critical Professor" and "Angry Protector" and "Skeptical Sam." This opened my eyes to how many voices were bouncing around in my head, arguing with one another on a daily basis. No wonder I couldn't figure out where to turn next!

With this kind of inner noise, how on earth could you hear yourself think? How on earth could you hear your own voice?

Chelsea wrote a book called *Negotiating the Inner Peace Treaty* that's all about how to get these voices to communicate with each other so you can finally get some relief.[1] It's full of exercises and questions that could easily be translated into writing assignments and used in conjunction with what you're learning here. But for the purposes of this book, and this chapter in particular, I want you to consider calling your one true voice of wisdom and joy your *narrator* voice.

## Narrators and Stories

To help you understand a little more about how a narrator operates in storytelling—and to help you make the connection to your own inner knowing and your writing—I need to explain a bit about how stories work. First of all, you need to know that stories have a clear beginning, middle, and end. Our lives, similarly, have a beginning (birth), a middle, and an end (death) but even more important, the stories within the greater stories of our lives follow this same structure. Every job you've ever had, relationship you've ever been a part of, or journey you've ever traveled has a beginning, middle, and an end.

Stories also usually follow a single character. The *protagonist* is the person we follow from the beginning of the story, through the messy middle, all the way to the end.

But the protagonist doesn't just simply move through the story; he or she is *changed* in the process. When we read a story where the main character doesn't change, we intuitively feel disappointed and confused. In fact, remember the last time you told a friend a story about your weekend, paused halfway through it, and thought to yourself, *Where was I going with this?* That's a story without a transformation. We call that a flat story. It's boring, it's hard to follow, and it's ultimately unsatisfying.

What I'm getting at is that while most of us understand that stories where the main character isn't going anywhere are boring, few of us have asked ourselves, *Where is my life going?*[2]

The narrator knows where the story is going. The narrator

knows who the main character is trying to become. Have you ever heard a narrator in a movie sound stressed or anxious? Neither have I. That's because the narrator knows things the protagonist does not know. Writing gives you access to this narrator voice inside you, a voice which is always present but sometimes gets overshadowed by the other voices.

What if you could hear the voice of your own inner narrator above the voices of the world around you—Instagram, your screaming children who need something from you, the neighbor who is critical or rude, your boss who never seems quite satisfied? What if you could hear your inner narrator more clearly than the critical voices from your past—your parents, your eighth-grade geometry teacher, your high school football coach?

If you've been lucky enough to have some helpful and encouraging voices in your life, you're at an advantage. But what if your narrator voice *still* knows something they don't know? Even the most well-meaning voices in our lives can give us advice that worked for them but gets us off track.

"Never go to bed angry . . ."
"You'll never make money being a writer . . ."
"Whatever you do, don't get a credit card . . ."
"Lean your head back when you get a nosebleed . . ."

I'm just listing out a few of the well-meaning pieces of advice I've been given by those who thought they were helping me. Their advice turned out to be either downright wrong, wrong for me, or just generally unhelpful and uninspiring. It has nothing to do with the intent of the speaker and everything to do with the value of a narrator voice. If you're the protagonist in your own story, who better to narrate than *your* narrator?

Your narrator voice knows more about you than anyone else

could. It knows who you are and where you're headed. It knows your deepest thoughts and feelings. It knows the beginning and the end. It knows the transformation you're after with such a certainty that it isn't phased in the slightest by the obstacles you face on the way. It knows this is all part of the plan.

Let me ask you this: do you believe you have an inner guide helping you along your journey and showing you where to go? Maybe you call this voice your intuition, or the "wisdom of the saints" or a still, small whisper, or the Holy Spirit. Whatever you call it, I'm calling it your narrator voice.

Perhaps you're uncertain or skeptical about this. If so, writing is a fantastic way to experiment and see if it's true for you. Write a question at the top of your paper, such as, "Where is my life headed?" or "What should I do next?" then free write for 10–20 minutes. See if you answer your own question.

I've worked with writers who swear they've practically "predicted the future" through their writing. They've written down things like where they're going to live or what they will be doing for a living in two years, only to stumble upon that time capsule years later. I found one recently that I'll share with you.

Back during the worst part of my divorce, a friend who is also a life coach suggested I write a present tense "diary entry" from my life five years in the future. She based this exercise on what she's learned about the power of visualization and its impact on our brains, the ability of subconscious thought to drive our behaviors, and even a few principals of hypnotherapy. It's similar to what I'm teaching you, albeit with a different lens.

I'm always up for this kind of stuff, so I took her up on her suggestion. The instructions were to choose a date a few years into the future, write the date at the top of the paper, and then write a "journal entry" as if I had already lived that day. I was forced, in other words, to imagine how things might be—where

I'd be living, what I'd be doing, and who I'd be with. The date I chose is still three months away from the day I'm writing this (meaning it hasn't even quite happened yet).

Below is a tiny segment of what I wrote:

"One of the things I love so much about this man I'm with is that he has the biggest heart of anyone I know. The *biggest* heart. He is always helping people and serving them and has given his entire life to the work he does, which means he's often on the road like I am. We don't get to be together all the time, but our reunions are sweet. You wouldn't believe what it does to your heart to always know that no matter what, you have a safe person and place to come home to. He is that safe place for me."

Obviously this paragraph could have just as easily been written today about my husband, Matt, and our life together. It feels almost eerie to read it. Everything I said about him in this entry was true—and I wrote it years before I ever knew who he was. How did I know?

To be candid, there are several things I wrote in that exercise that *didn't* come true. For example, I talked about waking our kids up for school—kids. Plural. While we do have a daughter on the way as I write this book, it will be a few more years before we have *kids* (plural)—or kids in school, for that matter. Maybe I was thinking I'd adopt someday. Maybe we still will. Maybe it was all just wishful thinking on my part.

The point is not that your narrator voice can predict every factual detail of your life (if it can, you have a new career path on your hands). The point is that your narrator voice—the most truthful and deepest part of you—*is* driving your life, whether you like it or not. So if, as you write, you find that your narrator voice is always whining and complaining about how life is unfair, you can expect that life is going to keep being pretty unfair. If you uncover a deep truth about yourself that you never realized—that, let's say, you're happiest when you're in the sunshine—don't be surprised if you end up moving away from Seattle!

This is not magical thinking or "woo woo" spirituality. This is neuroscience. Your buried thoughts and beliefs are driving your behavior.

Through writing, your narrator voice gives you access to what you really think and feel about the facts of your life. Can we predict outcomes? No. Can we have total control to shape them? Sorry, no. But your narrator voice does enable you to tap into the *truth* about your circumstances, so that you can change what *is* within your control: your response to your circumstances.

Your narrator voice can give you access to the part of yourself that is in tune with more than the daily struggles of your life. It can give you wisdom and perspective on the parts of your life that seem dark and confusing right now. Writing is like a portal or a passageway to this part of who you are. As you put words on the page, you'll suddenly begin to see, *This is who I am. This is what I want. This is why I'm here.*

Your narrator voice might just be your key to freedom.

## The Memoir of Your Life

Memoirs are, for obvious reasons, one of the easiest places to see narrator voice at work. You might have absolutely no desire to write a memoir of your life, now or ever—and that's perfectly reasonable. But go with this analogy for just a minute.

If you were to write a memoir of your life, what would the narrator of your story sound like, the voice that knows what's going to happen before it happens? I want you to stop and consider this. Imagine if you had a sit-down with your narrator, the wisest and most grounded part of yourself, and you summoned up the courage to ask, "What do I need to change in my life?" What would your narrator say to you? Would it say you're here to become more loving? To find courage? To stand up for someone else? To stand up for yourself? To come into your power? To use your gifts?

What if you were to ask the narrator to tell you the meaning of your life? Or where you are headed? What would your narrator say? If you were to imagine the final page or paragraph of your life story, what would be the takeaway?

Knowing what your narrator voice knows changes everything because it gives you context. Everything the protagonist experiences has meaning when we know the context of why he or she experiences it.

A woman who came to one of our Find Your Voice workshops—I'll call her Julie—was just learning to hear her narrator voice for the first time. Julie's sister was having an affair, and while this was supposed to be a big secret, in the small town where Julie and her sister lived, the secret was starting to leak out. Julie urged her sister to come clean about what was happening so that some resolution could be found, but no matter what she did or said, her sister wouldn't listen. Problems kept escalating as new people discovered the information and felt betrayed that they hadn't known earlier. And sure enough, to the sister and the rest of the family, Julie was always on speed dial. She was becoming exhausted.

Julie's mom begged Julie to convince her sister to end the affair. Julie's brother called her when he overheard the news at a local pub and wondered why Julie hadn't let him in on the situation earlier. Julie was half-worried that her brother-in-law was going to find out and show up at the house, furious with her for not talking sense into her sister.

To add another layer to the drama, Julie's family had rigid religious views that didn't feel like they fit Julie anymore. Julie told me that the shame and guilt her sister felt about what was happening and the choices she had made were intensified by her parents' insistence that staying married was the most important thing. Julie was sure this was a big reason why her sister felt so stuck. Oh, and by the way, Julie felt stuck right with her.

I walked Julie through *The Infinity Prompt*, and she wrote down all the facts of the situation, along with her own thoughts about the situation. She uncovered all kinds of biases and false narratives she was telling herself (i.e.: "If my sister would just ______, I could have my life back."). Then, at the end of the exercise, I asked Julie what her narrator would say about all of this.

Julie gave me a knowing look. It's the look of a writer when they realize they *know* the answer to their own question. She said, "The narrator would say, 'Julie had no idea that her sister's problems had nothing to do with her. She was not here to save them but to save herself.'"

*Not here to save her sister but to save herself.* That's a pretty profound insight. Thank you, narrator.

Sometimes the narrator's voice comes to us easily, and other times, it's more of a struggle. Sometimes you can sense the narrator's voice before you can actually hear it. Sometimes it shows up in sensations before it shows up in words. But this is why we keep writing about it. Because until it shows up in words, we have a hard time understanding what it's trying to tell us.

Another writer at a workshop—I'll call him Tim—told me he had come because he was worried about a friend who was consumed by addiction. Tim told me that 50 percent of the time, his friend was a total blast, the life of the party, and even a source of encouragement and support for him. But the other 50 percent of the time, this friend was erratic, irresponsible, unreliable, and sometimes even downright mean. In one of the writing prompts, Tim recounted a scenario wherein his friend actually slept with Tim's girlfriend, then mocked Tim for being upset about it.

I asked Tim what he thought the narrator might say about this story. Knowing the end of the story, and thinking of himself as the main character, what did the narrator know that Tim did not know? How could the narrator's perspective give Tim some perspective?

Tim wasn't sure. In fact, every time he thought about the "end," all he could think about was his friend ending up dead in a ditch somewhere. As hard as I knew it would be for Tim, I tried to get him to come back to *himself* as the main character of this story. His friend was a protagonist in a totally separate story, with his own decisions to make about where his life was heading—decisions that were literally life and death. But *Tim* was the protagonist in *Tim's* story. He was the one the "camera" was following. He was the one the audience was rooting for. He was the one whose transformation the "reader" was following.

So I asked Tim to consider what his own personal transformation might be. Tim still wasn't sure.

I challenged Tim to write again, but this time to write about himself in the third person. So the task was to write about the situation as if neither of them were his. There were two people in the story, Tim and the friend. Tim needed to write the story as if none of it was about him. This is when the epiphany came for him. To his own surprise and everyone else's, Tim wrote a scene wherein his friend was lying in a hospital bed, on the verge of death. In the scene, Tim was by his side, holding his hand. This is when Tim's narrator voice showed up.

As Tim wrote, he said a great peace came over him, and he knew beyond a shadow of a doubt that his friend was going to be okay. No matter what happened, he would be okay.

"He is safe," Tim's narrator told him. Somehow, just knowing that his friend was safe freed Tim to begin to think about his story as his own again, rather than thinking of himself as the "savior" in his friend's story. I asked Tim how he thought his life might change after all of this.

"I think I might start living for myself," he said.

Our narrator voices know things that we do not know. They know where we're headed. They know who we are. They possess a higher wisdom about the circumstances of our lives than we can access on our own. Writing down our stories, our thoughts, our ideas and our experiences can help us hear that voice.

## How Your Brain Responds to Your Narration

So far in this chapter, I've made this process sound quite mystical with the idea that some "higher" voice is inside of us, guiding us along our way. Perhaps there *is* some mysticism to this idea, but I would be remiss if I didn't also share what is happening in your brain as this higher, wiser part of you ends up on the page.

One thing we know to be true is that, as we begin to put language to our experiences—exactly what you're doing with the writing process—those experiences that used to cause us distress and discomfort lose their emotional control over us. Psychologists call the process of labeling these experiences "affect labeling."[3] They can actually track how, when you name a feeling, your brain becomes more active in the part responsible for control over your emotional state (the right prefrontal cortex) and less active in the part responsible for your body's fear response (the amygdala).[4]

In other words, the simple process of naming your emotional experience helps you regulate the emotion and move into the more logical, higher reasoning part of your brain. This is why kids who are throwing temper tantrums in the grocery store don't often turn to their mothers and say things like, "Mom, I'm exhausted and overwhelmed by all the stimulation in this place, which is why I'm acting overly distressed that you won't let me have that candy bar."* They simply don't have the language to understand their experience like that. But as adults, we *do* have the language.

The more *language* we have to name our emotional states, the more control we have over those powerful emotional states. This is the value of naming them. No *wonder* writing frees us up to think more clearly and come up with solutions to our own problems.

As Pennebaker states:

> When dealing with upsetting experiences, our working memory is reduced, and at the same time, our focus of attention is narrowed. We tend to think more narrowly and rigidly . . . [our] mindlessness . . . alleviate[s] the pain [of our emotional experience] at the cost of becoming *temporarily stupid*.[5]

Temporarily stupid is a great way to describe this state. If you've ever felt like that toddler in the grocery store—despite the fact that you are twenty-five or thirty-seven or sixty-two years old—then you know what I'm talking about. Perhaps you lost your temper with your child and got overly competitive or mean with a six-year-old. Maybe it was your spouse who tipped you over the edge, and you found yourself screaming or throwing things instead of using your words like the grown-up you are. Maybe you were stuck in rush hour traffic and found your usually calm and centered self flipping off the driver beside you and laying on your horn.

If you have ever felt "temporarily stupid," you're not alone. Have you considered that it might not be because you're *actually*

---

* If your children do this, please send parenting advice.

stupid? It might be because the emotional response you're having to a particular circumstance—the lawsuit that's been filed against you, the fact that your wife unexpectedly left this summer, the pregnancy you lost last month, or the sexual trauma you've never talked about—might be inhibiting your ability to think clearly and problem-solve. Writing about it and labeling your experience might free you up to access the wisest and most thoughtful part of yourself.

Dr. Pennebaker commented on how some of his research participants experienced emotional relief through their writing process:

> When people were asked why writing had helped them, many spontaneously said that they came to a new understanding of the emotional events themselves. Problems that had seemed overwhelming became simpler and more manageable after seeing them on paper. Writing helped to resolve problems. Once the issues were resolved, there was no need to think about them anymore.[6]

As you write down the events and experiences of your life, you begin to rise above them—just as you would if you were "lifting" above your house in that hot air balloon. Writing helps you do this. It helps you clear your mind, resolve the questions that keep you up at night, gain some sense of direction and answers, metabolize all of the new data and experiences that are coming your way, and do so in a way that you can be honest and free and open without drastic consequences.

## The Tasks of Life

Some clients have expressed to me that when they start getting into the thick of the writing process, the experience starts to feel self-indulgent, and they wonder what on earth qualifies them to be the narrator of their own lives. I remind them that life is complicated and that as hard as it is to own our choices and shape our experiences, it is the only way to the freedom and happiness we crave.

I want to turn back to Pennebaker's work one last time, because his thoughtful conclusions on the challenges of life and writing can help us contextualize *why* "self-indulgent" should be the last word we use to describe this process:

> Consider what researchers found to be some of the more common life tasks that we set for ourselves: to love and to be loved; to make the world a better place; to raise healthy and happy children; to succeed professionally and financially; to be honest with ourselves and with others. As if these tasks were not difficult enough to accomplish, imagine the problems we face when confronted with an overwhelming trauma.[7]

If writing (and life) seem complicated and overwhelming, that's because they *are*. That's because you are paying close attention. It's because you care. If you didn't, you wouldn't be here. You would not have made it this far. You'd be doing something much simpler than digging into the thoughts and feelings that are guiding your life through writing. If you've suffered a trauma and you're doing this work, you deserve a medal. This is a herculean effort. Your efforts will shift the course of your life forever.

No matter who you are, there is a voice inside you that is truer than the voices you hear most of the day. It is truer than your everyday ego, the self that judges you for not getting things quite right, the self that judges other people for not getting it quite right. There is a voice that is more trustworthy than that voice. Perhaps you are very familiar with this voice, or perhaps you've had relatively little contact with this part of yourself. Either way, writing can help you hear the voice that can be your lifeline.

Whatever you call it, it's there for the same purpose—to guide you and comfort you. It has a wealth of great wisdom and joy. Most of us are not nearly as familiar with this voice as we are with all the other voices in our life.

Perhaps it's time we got to know each other better.

CHAPTER 10

# The Passage of Time

## How long this takes and a call to keep going

It was November 2016, about ten days before the presidential election. Emotions were running higher than ever as the final vote boiled down to Donald Trump and Hillary Clinton. The country was as divided as ever. Republicans were calling Hillary a liar, Democrats were calling Trump a misogynist, and the general sentiment I was hearing from many people was that it was a terrifying and uncertain time. No matter which way you hoped the vote would go, none of us could deny that things were about to be different. All of us held our breath and wondered what on earth was going to happen next.

For months, during the early primaries, my friends and I had been saying there was no way Trump would make it to the final election. So now that we had arrived, I was feeling as stunned as anyone. To add insult to injury, I was newly divorced, newly freed from what had been a controlling and abusive relationship. I was just barely getting my "sea legs," as a friend of mine would say.

All this to say, I needed Trump to *not* be president. I don't mean that in a political way, although we could also have that conversation. What I mean is that I'd been traumatized by a man who'd controlled my every move and monitored every word out of my mouth and edited every word I put on paper for over four years, now I was *finally* free of that whole mess, and I needed it not to be Trump who was elected. I needed the new president, on a very visceral and personal level, to be someone else.

Anyone else.

Maybe this was the tipping point that prompted me to book a little cabin down by the beach on the Gulf Coast of Florida to get away from the whole mess. I decided I was going to write out my whole story. The story of my divorce. I'd already mapped it out. I had written a handful of pieces. Writing was one of a few ways I coped during the dismantling of my life. I wrote down little snippets to help me remember the facts and details of the situation. I wrote to remind myself what I thought or how I felt about things, since I would still get confused—a symptom of gaslighting.

Sometimes I felt like a deep fog had settled in around my brain, and I would sit down to write, and the fog would lift for a minute.

So I booked myself a little oasis by the water in Seagrove, Florida and brought nothing much with me beyond my laptop and a pair of running shoes. The cabin wasn't much. It looked like it had been decorated in the 1980s with a beach theme—complete with seashell wallpaper—and not updated much since. But the most beautiful part of this place—all I needed, really—were the sliding doors that opened right up to the ocean.

That is where I sat to write. I kept the door open so I could hear the waves crashing over each other and smell the healing, salty air. My fingers literally flew over the keys during those eight days. Sometimes words come quickly, and sometimes they come slowly. But in this case, the words came fast, and I let them come.

You'll remember the promise I made to myself about this story: that I was going to tell the truth. The whole ugly truth. I wasn't going to hold anything back anymore. So I let the words flow through my heart and into my fingertips like a flood, and come they did. That's when something unexpected happened.

I thought that writing down every detail of my story would make me feel better. I thought there would be a sense of catharsis—I had witnessed this with so many of my clients. They'd come, they'd work with me, and they'd leave feeling like a wave of relief and clarity had come over them. I had experienced it a hundred times myself. But this time was different. Relief and clarity were the furthest thing from what I felt.

Instead, I felt darkness settle in around me like a thick cloud of smoke. I felt grief like I had never felt before. I sobbed as I typed the words on the screen. Every so often, I would stand up, go for a walk on the beach so I could breathe for a moment, and come back to the worst part: none of it was publishable. I wouldn't have shown it to my mother, let alone a publisher.

The words, to be frank, felt as dark as I felt in that condo at the beach. Some of them were downright mean and vindictive. Some of them, as I read them back to myself, were petty and whiney. I sounded like a pouting teenage girl. I was a thirty-three-year-old woman, for goodness sake! What was my problem?

But still, for reasons I didn't understand at the time but do now, I let the words come. I tried not to judge or evaluate or edit, but instead to just write and trust that whatever I was writing knew what it wanted to be more than I did. Write now, edit later. It wasn't easy. I wanted to give up a thousand times. But I held the space for the words that needed to come out.

Only later would I see why it was good that I did.

## What Time Doesn't Heal

You've heard it said that time heals all wounds, but this is categorically untrue. Not only does time *not* heal all wounds, but time has a way of cementing into place patterns and habits that were at one time our saving grace (things like lying, or drinking, or pushing away anyone who gets close to us) but are now painful and self-destructive. These may have been patterns or behaviors that protected us or even saved our lives at one point or another. But later, they become the very thing that tears us apart.

You can probably think of someone in your life right now who has patterns of behavior like this—solidified over the passage of time—that are toxic to their very existence. Maybe that person is you.

Why would anyone who has demolished their life, their family, and their body through the use of alcohol, for example, keep picking up the bottle? Or why would a woman who has broken free from a toxic relationship where she's controlled, belittled, and even beaten take her lover back? Why would someone who has been diagnosed with lung cancer keep picking up a cigarette?

Are we gluttons for punishment? Or have the wounds of our past "healed" in such a way that they aren't actually healed at all? Have they calcified into defense mechanisms and coping protocols that keep us from feeling pain but are ultimately stealing our mental and emotional well-being?

Why do we set resolutions or declare we're going to change our lives and not do it? Why do we have beautiful dreams and intentions and not live up to them? The answers are multi-faceted and perhaps too numerous to unpack in this book. But I want to point out that the overarching answer to all of these questions is time does *not* heal all wounds. Without careful reflection, attention, committed action, and—sometimes—trained help, these patterns in our lives don't change. In fact, they continue getting more deeply ingrained and detrimental.

Dr. Joe Dispenza puts it this way in his book, *Breaking the Habit of Being Yourself*:

> If you've been devoted to feeling negatively for years, those feelings have created an automatic state of being. We could say that you are subconsciously unhappy, right? Your body has been conditioned to be negative; it knows how to be unhappy better than your conscious mind knows otherwise. You don't even have to think about how to be negative. You just know that's how you are. How can your conscious mind control this attitude in the subconscious body-mind?[1]

And here's the part from Dispenza that really gets me . . .

> I want to be clear that, by itself, *positive thinking never works*. Many so-called positive thinkers have felt negative most of their lives, and now they're trying to think positively. They are in a polarized state in which they are trying to think one way in order to override how they feel inside of them . . . *When the mind and body are in opposition, change will never happen.*[2]

What he's saying here is that if you tend to feel negatively about the world, yourself, your relationships, or your challenges, most likely it's because this negative state is memorized in your body and your brain. Not only that, but positive thinking won't even touch that memorized state! Positive thinking can't help because time (even with great optimism) can't heal all wounds.

So if time doesn't heal all wounds, then what *does* heal them? My theory would be *awareness*. Careful reflection and attention to our behavior and our bodies is the only way they ever change. And writing is an absolutely foolproof way to curate awareness. You cannot write for long and not see yourself show up on the page.

Dr. Pennebaker says,

> We are often surprisingly ignorant of our needs, motivations and conflicts. When out of control, anxious or upset, we naturally change our thinking style. Although low-level thinking can reduce our pain, it can also narrow our thinking to such an extent that we fail to see that something is the matter. We can then become the central feature of our self-constructed paradox: if we naturally escape from the knowledge that something is wrong, how can we ever know about it? How can we ever hope to control the problem or change our lives?[3]

The question Pennebaker poses here is an important one for us to turn on ourselves: *How can we ever hope to change if we don't know how or why or even* that *we need to change?* We cannot heal our wounds until we understand them.

Writing helps us begin that work.

What was happening to me at the beach as I wrote my book was the same thing that has happened to the hundreds of authors and "not real" writers who have trusted me with their stories and their writing process over time: we were cultivating awareness. We were starting to see things more clearly. We were standing outside of our stories, outside of our circumstances, and seeing them from a new perspective.[4]

The great thing about this is that awareness is the beginning of change. In fact, in therapeutic models of change, the step *before* the first step is called *precontemplation*. Precontemplation is the stage wherein the person who needs to change hasn't even recognized the problem yet. This is the addict who won't admit they're an addict. It's the battered woman who swears the bruises are from falling down the stairs. It's the moment on the scale when you swear to yourself the extra ten pounds are your clothes.

We'd rather pretend the scale is broken, sometimes, than

recognize that where we are is not where we want to be. This is precontemplation.

The stage that comes after precontemplation is predictable. It's *contemplation*. The dictionary definition of contemplation is, "The action of looking thoughtfully at something *for a long time*."

*For a long time*. I want you to keep this in your mind as you read the rest of this chapter.

The great thing about awareness is that it ushers us into the change process. The terrible part about awareness, as enacted through the stage of contemplation, is that it involves going back into our pain to look at it and sit with it and notice it—*for a long time*. This is not a quick fix or a magic pill or a mood stabilizing drug. Somewhere along the way, we got the impression that we should never have to feel any pain at all, so we learned to numb our pain. But pain is not inherently bad. Pain just points us toward what's wrong.

What would it look like for you to go back and sit with your pain? To look at it? To relive it? What about sitting with it *for a long time*? For me, that looked like eight days at the beach, alone, recounting the story of my marriage and divorce. For you, it might look different, but I'm asking you to consider how writing could play a role.

The research is clear: writing can help us manage negative emotional states, process our lives, and even heal from trauma. One of the reasons writing does this, I believe, is because it invites us, and even requires us, to look at our pain in a new way and for a long time. It requires *contemplation*.

This process of sitting with your pain is the very reason writing can heal your life, and it's the very reason you'll avoid it. You're at a crossroads here. You get to choose between staying comfortable but stuck in the same old loops and pushing through discomfort to your own breakthrough.

For many of us—myself included—sitting down to write about the pain we've faced will be the first time we've ever looked at it up close. Even when we *lived through it*, we didn't really look at it. We can't survive and contemplate at the same time, so we survived by pretending the pain wasn't happening, by numbing out, by talking ourselves out of the sensations we felt in our bodies, by the very habits and coping mechanism I've already mentioned, and by doing the *opposite* thing writing teaches us to do: show up and look at what's actually going on.

There's a saying in my family that goes, "If it looks like chocolate, and it tastes like chocolate, then it's chocolate." Meaning we have to stop fooling ourselves into thinking that things are not what we *know* they are. We have to stop willfully ignoring the facts of a situation, trying to pretend we don't feel the things we feel, trying to protect people who haven't earned our protection, and being unwilling to admit to ourselves that we would like the circumstances of our lives to be different.

Having a "positive attitude" can be great, but not when the positivity is dishonest. Remember what Dr. Joe Dispenza wrote? You can't cover negativity with positivity and pray it helps. When your sister has cancer, you can't pretend she doesn't have it and expect her to get better. If your friend has a drinking problem, ignoring it won't make it go away. If there's a pattern in your life that plays out over and over again, you cannot "positive affirmation" your way out of it. You have to face the facts of the situation. You have to face your feelings about it. You have to unpack and understand the thoughts that got you here, and identify the thoughts that will get you out.

You are going to have to look at the situation, look at it honestly, and look at it *for a long time*. Writing can help you do all of this.

But only if you have the courage to stay with it.

## Tiny Blades of Hope

A few months before Matt and I got married, some landscapers came to our house and planted grass seed in our backyard. I grew up in Oregon, so what I'm about to tell you felt foreign to me at the time, but now that I live in California, I've realized that when you don't water your yard (because, let's say, you turn off the sprinklers to conserve water in a drought), the grass dies. Who knew? Since Matt and I were getting ready to host our rehearsal dinner in our backyard, we decided we wanted to get the grass looking extra lush.

Knowing the countdown was on, Matt called the landscapers right away. They tore out the remaining patches of barely alive grass, tilled the soil, fertilized the whole thing, and then put down grass seed. At the end of it all, Matt and I looked at what used to be a sad-looking joke of a lawn and realized that now, the entire thing looked even *worse*, and smelled like a pile of manure to top it off. With only thirty days until the wedding, we looked at our yard and then at each other.

Had we just made a terrible mistake?

The landscaper in charge of the crew assured us that we'd have no problem getting the grass to fully grow in by the day of our rehearsal dinner. We must have recounted the date to him three different times—even interrupting him as he explained how to operate the sprinklers. We said it a different way each time, just to make sure he understood. We could not believe that in thirty days, this *manure* pile was going to be presentable enough for a rehearsal dinner.

We watched that backyard like hawks. Every morning we woke up and walked to the back windows, which were conveniently in the kitchen, near the coffee. We pulled back the curtains and peeked to see if any grass was coming up. Day after day after day we did this. A week passed, and there was nothing. Then another week. Still nothing. We started making contingency plans.

But then, right around the two-week mark, Matt woke up one morning and went to make the coffee. He pulled back the curtains like he usually did. That's when I heard him shout from the other room.

"Babe! Come look at this!"

I stumbled to the kitchen. Matt was already in the backyard—barefoot—staring at what I *hoped* was grass (because otherwise . . . *weird*). I followed his lead, hands wrapped around my warm coffee cup, and we both knelt down on the deck together. Sure enough, there they were in all their glory. Thousands upon thousands of tiny blades of grass.

Those first two weeks felt excruciatingly *long* as we waited for the grass to pop up and show its friendly face. We had resigned ourselves to the possibility that it might not come. See how much we rely on our sense? To know something is true, we want to *see* it.

Once those tiny sprouts popped up, the grass actually grew quite quickly. Or maybe it was at the same pace, but now that we could see it, it seemed faster. Either way, it appeared that every single day, when we woke up and pulled back those curtains, there were more blades of grass, and they were thicker and taller and fuller and longer. Finally, a week before the wedding, the landscaper had to come back and mow the grass. That's how lush it was.

Here's what I realized after this episode of trusting, waiting, panicking, and finally seeing: the early stages of growth happen *under the surface*. This is true of grass, and it is true of writing, true of discovering the message we want to share with our lives. No, time does not heal all wounds. But when we plant something new and give it a little bit of water and nurture and patient attention, over time, we do see the threads of hope show up. Things *do* change. It doesn't happen overnight, but it happens. And one day, we wake up and see that after all that waiting, things are actually quite lush.

## How Long Will This Take?

Writers and those who still swear they're not writers always want to know how long this will take, and I have to give them an honest answer: I do not know for sure, but probably a long time.

I did eventually finish my memoir about getting out of an abusive marriage. It's called *Indestructible: Leveraging Your Broken Heart to Become a Force of Love and Change in the World.* I often talk about how I wrote the book in ten days to demonstrate how books come at the pace they want to come, and also to show how operating with a working outline frees up your brain to write much faster.

But it also feels important to mention that the 60,000 words I left the beach with after those ten days are not the same 55,000 words or so that ended up in the book. I had to practice what I preach: write now, edit later.

In fact, that manuscript sat on my computer untouched for over twelve months before I opened it again. It needed time, like good coffee or cheese or grass seed growing under the surface. You cannot rush these things. I needed time to let things unfold and transpire in my life before I was ready to share those tender shoots of grass with anyone else. Twelve months later, when I finally did open that file tucked away in my laptop, I spent about a month editing.

Do you want to know something predictable as well as life-changing? I came back to my story twelve months later with an entirely new perspective. With the passage of time and a little more awareness, how could I not see the story of my marriage and divorce differently than I had when my mind and body were still living *in* that traumatic situation?

I call this life-changing because it is. I didn't spend every hour of every day thinking about the words I had written. In fact, I can't say I thought of those words much at all as they sat buried in my laptop. Maybe a handful of times, if I had to count. It wasn't as if I was constantly wondering what themes I should include or how to get my narrator voice just right.

Do you know what pushed me back to the document again? I met a man who was kind, loyal, and a wonderful friend to me. Things felt different. Suddenly I started thinking I wanted to edit. So I pulled out my laptop and opened the document, and all of a sudden, things that used to be confusing seemed clear. The details of the story hadn't changed, but the framing of it—the way I told my story to myself—had. The facts of the story never changed, but my feelings and thoughts did. The way we tell our stories matters—especially the way we tell them to ourselves. I noticed different details this time. My narrator voice was in full force. And as my story changed, my life changed with it.

This is not just true for me but for hundreds of my clients. Our experiences are validated and backed up by research. Awareness changes things. It's not only discipline or effort or willpower or efficiency or productivity that brings progress, but also a gentle noticing of yourself. Contemplation. Looking at a thing for a long time.

As we take this journey together, it feels only responsible for me to warn you that the kind of change you hope to see in your life—the kind I have seen in mine—is going to take what feels like an absurd amount of time. It will not *be* absurd—and you'll see progress in as little as four days—but it is likely to *feel* absurd because we live in a world that can deliver just about anything we want to us in under sixty minutes. Even something beautiful or special.

On the street corner the other day, in Pasadena where I live, there was a man offering to write a customized poem for me, on any topic of my choice, in under ten minutes. Just an hour before that, I had an assortment of hand-pressed juices delivered to my door in a matter of thirty-five minutes with the click of a button on my phone. And that's during morning rush hour in LA!

So we have to remind ourselves, before we enter into a process that is delicate and sometimes can feel quite slow, that not all things in life can be ordered with the click of a button on our smartphones. Emotional healing is not delivered through Amazon Prime.* In fact, the best things in life grow slowly: relationships, children, careers, the oak tree in your backyard, and your writing practice. Think of it like a garden. Get started now, so that in a few months, you will have something to eat.

The reason I bring this up is so that when the feeling inevitably comes up that this is taking too long, you'll remember these words and you won't give up. You are about to get to the good stuff. The worst mistake you could make is to get days or weeks into this, worry you aren't making any progress, and decide to move onto something more efficient and productive. That is a choice you will later regret, I know from experience.

One of the main reasons we struggle so much with *creativity* is that the culture we live in is obsessed with *productivity*. We want to see a measurable return for every single minute we spend working toward something. Unfortunately, this measuring metric is contradictory to the human soul and how it operates. The paths that offer the most "progress" to the soul—therapy, art, dance, music, writing, yoga, meditation—cannot be taken without wandering and dead ends and failures and blank space and plenty of things that feel like a waste of time.

---

* At least not the last time I checked.

The other day, I spoke with a potential author who told me he was calling because publishers keep reaching out to him, telling him it's time to write. He has a public platform, and publishers see an opportunity there. They know he can sell books. He assured me he has no "illusions" about his own ability to write, that he's not a "real writer" and that he's a very busy man with no time to write. He told me that if he was going to work on a book, he would need lots of help and a guarantee that it was going to have a strong ROI.

I was getting ready to tell him I wasn't the coach for him because when you start using words like "return on investment" to talk about your writing, I worry that all the best benefits of writing will be lost on you.

I started easing into it, saying, "Some authors call me because they have a story nagging at them that won't leave them alone. Now, this doesn't sound like you, but some authors talk about waking up in the middle of the night . . ."

At that, I heard his voice break on the other end of the phone. There was a long pause. His breathing picked up a little bit, and I was almost certain I could hear him crying. When he finally spoke again, he said something I was both shocked and also not shocked at all to hear .

He said, "That's me. I do have a story I need to tell. It's about me as a little boy . . ."

Under the surface, I believe we all have a story we're dying to tell. It's tapping at the door. Softly, at times, and at other times not so gently. We find ways to ignore it—busy schedules and emails and Instagram. But it doesn't leave us alone forever. It wants to be heard. It *needs* to be heard. It's on a mission to wake us up to ourselves.

The human soul does not crave productivity the way the human mind does. The human soul craves depth, not width.

The human soul couldn't give two rips about ROI. The human soul is concerned with contribution, legacy, impact, generosity, and value. The human soul is much more concerned with what it can give than what it can get. The human soul wants to understand who it is and why it's here.

Are you telling your soul to sit down and shut up so you can do the "more important" work of getting through the week? Many of us are, and to our own great detriment.

Writing is not a golden ticket or a magic pill. But facing a blank page—exactly because it is difficult—is a tool, proven by science, to bring us back into alignment with ourselves. You can't write for very long and not see the truth of yourself on the page. You can avoid it for a long time but not forever. Deciding to let go is as simple (and as terrifying) as putting another day's words on the page.

CHAPTER 11

# Write It Like a Love Letter

## Why giving your writing the right destination unlocks your words

My friends and family joke that I have a special talent for getting people to tell me their deepest truths within ten minutes of knowing them. Just the other night, I was mingling at a party when a line of questions I asked led one woman in the group to tell me a dark story from her past.

"I don't even know why I'm telling you this," she said. "You're a total stranger."

According to Pennebaker, disclosure is a *huge* reason why writing is such a powerful tool for healing and growth. Secrets kill. Literally. Keeping secrets is physical work.

"When we try to keep secrets, we must actively hold back or inhibit our thoughts, feelings, or behaviors. Keeping secrets from others means that we must consciously restrain, hold back, or in some way exert effort to not think, feel or behave."[1]

Still, studies show most of us are keeping secrets. Lots of them. One study I read showed that 90 percent of kids have grasped the concept of lying by age four, and that it gets worse from there.[2] We lie about all kinds of mundane and unimportant things, from what we ate for breakfast to whether or not we've seen that popular movie. We lie to make ourselves look better, to "fit in," and on any given day, the average person is keeping about thirteen secrets, five of which they consider "big" secrets.[3] Things they'd be *terrified* to have anyone find out.

But lying is not just a cute, benign thing we do. Forget the fact that truth is a virtue for just a second, and focus on the fact that lying and keeping secrets has a long-term impact on our physical, emotional, and mental health. The less often we put words to the emotional events that happen to us, the more likely that emotional experience is to have a negative impact on our lives. Holding back what wants to be expressed in us and through us impairs our bodies, our spirits, and our minds.

Lying and keeping secrets can also impact our cognitive abilities. When you're keeping a secret—when you have something to say or express that you feel you cannot say or express—your brain doesn't work very well. You lose things, forget things, get lost easily, and generally have a harder time listening and processing information. Perhaps this is why traumatized students don't tend to perform well and get lower grades, statistically.

Several studies I read presented evidence that secrets take physical work and make us tired. One researcher speculated about why this is: "One of the main reasons for the negative effect on energy level and performance is because secrets make us feel lonely and sad. They also can make us feel more fearful, hostile, and guilty, but sadness and isolation make us more tired."[4]

Okay, so secrets make us not just tired, but also lonely, sad, hostile, and guilty. This is why disclosure helps so much. Pennebaker writes, "When disclosing deeply personal experiences, there are immediate changes in brain activation, skin conductance levels and overt behavioral correlates to the letting go experience."[5]

There's only one problem. Disclosure to the wrong person, or at the wrong time, can be dangerous.

Imagine a woman telling her abusive husband that she's been cheating on him, not knowing how he will react. Imagine a daughter telling her mother that her father—her mother's husband—has been molesting her since she was a baby. If her mom responds by validating her claim and getting her daughter to safety, then disclosure will be helpful for her. If not, it can be tragic.

Think for a moment about our current cultural attitude about "being authentic" and "telling the truth" online. Is it helpful to tell your most tender secrets to your Instagram following? Or does it open you up to damaging criticism and unhelpful feedback before you are ready for it? The answer is left, mostly, up to chance.

So if secrets kill but disclosure can be dangerous, what do we do? Enter *expressive writing*.

What happens when we write down an experience that was traumatic for us is that we translate the event into language. Whether you're processing a traumatic event from years ago, or you're digesting an experience that is happening in the moment, writing is a way to disclose and translate these events into language so that they don't have a long-term negative effect on you.

When there are no safe places in our lives for us to disclose an event, or when we aren't sure who or where those safe places are, writing is an incredible tool that gives us the freedom language brings. Writing can help us break the control that our stories often have over us.

Maybe you have a secret to tell but nowhere safe to disclose it. Perhaps writing can be the very first safe place for you to share.

## Don't Show Your Work

Do you remember that really annoying thing you had to do in high school math class? *Show your work*, the teacher would say.

Meaning, show your steps in the process. That way, if you got to the wrong answer, they could see where you got hung up. If you got to the *right* answer, the teacher could make sure you hadn't just copied them all out of the answers section in the back of the book.

I have great news for you about the writing process. You never *ever* have to show your work.

To me, this is what makes writing such a unique form of processing and healing. There's a sense of privacy inherent in the work. As you use words to name your complicated experiences, you can try one word, and if it doesn't work, scratch it out and try a new one. You never have to worry you've led someone astray by using the wrong word. Nobody has seen it. Nobody will ever see it. Most of what we write ends up in the garbage can.

If you were processing these things out loud—putting language to them by telling a friend—you'd have to deal with the possible repercussions of judgment, criticism, or even social isolation as you tried out one idea before moving on to another. Not with writing. On the blank page, you have full permission to test out a thought or idea, and then delete it if it doesn't fit.

Many people don't have anywhere safe, stable, or private where they can share what's really on their minds. If you do have a place like this, consider yourself lucky. If you don't, I have great news for you: you can create this kind of environment inside yourself. It isn't easy, and it doesn't come overnight. But it *is* possible. Writing will help you do it.

How can writing become a place where you feel safe to express yourself? How can you create an inner environment where you feel free? Could you do something to your physical space? Could you burn your writing when it was done? What if you wrote a few pages and never even went back and read it—would that make you feel safe?

See if you can find a way to make your own mind the safest place you have ever lived. And then, I dare you to see if the world around you doesn't start to feel a little safer as well.

## Write It Like a Love Letter

To keep you motivated and prevent you from getting stuck, I'm going to teach you a trick I teach even to writers who want to publish. It goes like this: write it like a love letter.

Writing it like a love letter is about taking your eyes off the crowd and determining one person, a real person, who is going to be the "imaginary" recipient of your writing. Writing to one specific person solves two problems. First, it solves the feeling that your writing is going nowhere. And second, it has a way of taking us off the "stage" we put ourselves on and into that safe, stable, private environment. You might not consider yourself an "onstage" sort of person, but think about all of the roles you play where you are required, in a sense, to perform a certain way.

As a parent, you're playing the role of the loving, stable, secure provider. As a spouse, you're playing the role of the supportive, optimistic, committed partner. As an employee, you're playing the role of the productive, cooperative, empathetic leader. Now, I'm not suggesting that these things are not true of you. I'm only suggesting that sometimes it can be nice to *step off the stage* for a minute and say something that's honest but doesn't fit one of those roles.

For example, in writing an imaginary journal entry to their boss, a writer might feel free to admit that they are actually quite unhappy with their job, or that they have a coworker who is a huge problem. As far as actually disclosing this information to their boss is concerned, they can make that decision later, but it is helpful for them to express how they truly feel.

One writer who thought she had fallen out of love with her

husband found herself admitting, in an imaginary letter to him, that she was more in love with him than ever. In fact, she found herself telling him that she had felt his distance lately and was terrified of losing him. Her disconnection was a defense mechanism. This was a revelation to her—and it came about because she gave her writing a destination. This is the power of writing it like a love letter.

The tool of writing it like a love letter is designed to get you to the place where you can tell the truth, and tell it in a loving, present, visceral way.

Maybe you write your next entry to your spouse. Maybe to your son. Maybe to your mother. Or maybe to the man you ran into on the street the other day who has—for some unknown reason—captured your attention. Maybe you write to a loved one who has passed on. The point is to step off the "stage" we so often tend to stand on in our lives, let down our guard, and write it like a letter to someone we love.

Where it used to feel like you didn't know how to say what you needed to say, now you are beginning to know. Where it once seemed like you weren't sure what details to include and which ones to leave out, now it's coming into focus. Where you used to feel under-motivated, now maybe you feel a small spark of inspiration.

*Love* is a complicated word. But writing to someone you love *will* move you in the direction of love. Love for yourself. Love for others. Love for the world. No matter what you choose, love will be what drives you. It will be what fuels you. When it's challenging to get the words down, you'll remember love.

When you do this, a magical thing happens. Your writing suddenly becomes richer. You have more and better raw material to work with. You're not stuck anymore. These are the beautiful, juicy, delicious ingredients of your life.

CHAPTER 12

# The Ending That Hasn't Been Written

## The myth about endings and how to get a "happily ever after"

There's a moment I've come to expect whenever I'm helping a new writer outline their personal story. It happens at around three-fourths of the way through the process, and it's so predictable now that I can almost time it. They look at the story, and realize the ending hasn't happened yet.

You might be thinking, *Of course, the ending hasn't happened yet. We're still* alive. But as you write the smaller stories of your life (the story of getting fired, going through a divorce, having a baby) think about how often we "write" the ends of stories in our minds before they have been written.

You'd be shocked (or maybe not shocked at all) to know the number of people who decide their love life is over when they go through a break-up, or that their career is ruined forever because of one bad decision, or that they'll never be a parent because they haven't become one by thirty-five. We have an unhelpful and also completely normal tendency to "finish" the story before it's really finished.

Maybe it's because we don't like lingering in that space between the questions and the answers. The mystery feels like too much for us.

Remember the story I told you earlier about the virus that was spreading rapidly across the globe—the coronavirus? Now, just a few weeks later, the virus has turned into what we'll know forever as COVID-19, a global pandemic. Cities and states are in lockdown. Businesses are closed. People are dying. It remains to be seen how this will all end. The whole world waits in anticipation. The uncertainty is deafening.

I feel myself at moments wanting to "write the ending" to this global pandemic before it's been written. I see this tendency in others as well. We say things like, "This is all going to be fine," or "Two million people are going to die!" Really? Is that true? How do you know? I've heard people say *both* that we'll never recover from this *and* that this is all going to "blow over" in a few days. Each of these assertions, while different in ways, are the same desperate attempt to get resolution. The truth is, none of us know. And not knowing is hard to handle.

This is what I want you to keep in mind during this chapter, as we talk about the endings of our stories, both "endings" in the broader sense—as in, the ends of our lives—and also the endings of the smaller stories in our lives. I want you to think about the end of a marriage story or a job story or the end of the current season you're in: raising young children or finishing school or a time of loneliness. I want you to remember that you cannot finish the story before it's finished. In fact, if you are willing to stay *in* the story *right where you* are by writing about it, you get to participate in the resolution.

Maybe you're in the middle of a confusing story right now.

Maybe you're wondering about the health and safety of a loved one. Maybe you're wondering if your small business will survive. It's painful to sit and wait and wonder what's going to happen. It's painful to stay in the story when we don't know.

But the reason we write our stories while we are in them is that it helps us to see more clearly. When we map out a story the way an author maps out a memoir, it helps us see where we are in the story right now. It helps us expand our ideas about how the story might end. And it helps us move in the direction we would most like to go.

## How Stories Resolve

To think a story needs to resolve "perfectly" in order to resolve at all is a terrible mistake that will keep you from resolving your own story through the art of writing it down. Stories do not resolve perfectly, and when they do, we usually don't trust the resolution. Think of the last time you rolled your eyes at the end of a movie because the resolution was too trite for you. All of the main character's problems and questions were probably wrapped up in one terribly cliché climactic scene.

This is called lazy storytelling. This is what makes you leery of thinking ahead of time about the resolution to the story that you're living right now. Your brain rightly reminds you that life isn't a movie. And your brain is right; it's not! But what if the greatest endings ever written were nuanced, just like you are?

When you start to look at the endings of stories in the books you love most, you will find that actually endings are *usually* quite nuanced. Take the ending of the *New York Times* bestselling memoir *Hillbilly Elegy* by J. D. Vance. The memoir depicts the author's struggles growing up as a member of the white working class, and how he rose above the circumstances of his upbringing to create a meaningful life. The last paragraph of the last chapter reads:

> I got out of bed for a glass of cold water, and when I returned, Casper was staring at me, wondering what on earth this human was doing awake at such an odd hour. It was two o' clock in the morning—probably about the same time it was when I first woke from that terrifying dream over twenty years earlier. *There was no Mamaw to comfort me.* But there were my two dogs on the floor, and there was the love of my life lying in bed. Tomorrow I would go to work, take the dogs to the park, buy groceries with Usha and make a nice dinner. It was everything I ever wanted. So I patted Casper's head and went back to sleep.[1]

What better picture could there be of the simplicities and tensions of real life? Our loved ones are not always there to comfort us. But even in their absence, we have enough. We have the simple joys of pets and beds and groceries and loved ones and dinner.

Or what about Barbara Kingsolver's *The Poisonwood Bible*, the powerful and tragic story of a family's journey to be evangelical missionaries in Africa in the 1950s? The father in the story is a complicated character—an overzealous Baptist minister who drags his wife and daughters across the world to bring the gospel to the "unenlightened" souls of Africa. Throughout the story, it becomes more and more clear how misguided his mission has always been. The entire mess is told through the lens of this man's wife and five daughters.

The final paragraph of the book is narrated by Ruth May, who died thanks to her father's rash choices. She offers this forgiveness:

> I do. I think of [my father] exactly this way. We are the balance of our damage and our transgressions. He was my father. I own half his genes, and all of his history. Believe this: *the mistakes*

> *are part of the story.* I am born of a man who believed he could tell nothing but the truth, while he set down for all time The Poisonwood Bible.[2]

The mistakes are part of the story. Talk about the hard-won wisdom of putting down your complicated, beautiful, compassionate, and tragic story on paper. This is not a trite and cliché ending that haphazardly ties up the loose ends. This is the work of an author who has fought to untie the knots of her history so she can have just a tiny bit better perspective on them. And we're so glad she did it.

Talk about narrator voice.

And finally, take a look at the ending to my own challenging story of leaving an abusive relationship and restarting my life from scratch. In the story, by this point, I've lost everything. My home. My dog. My marriage. My business. Even, in ways, the faith of my upbringing. I've been guided through the treacherous journey by an eccentric friend and yoga instructor named Sarah. And somehow, with her guidance and my own participation, I've been able to find the most beautiful measure of hope:

> As I stood by the ocean, doing the moves in the only way I knew how, I started to feel like maybe everything was going to be okay. No matter what came next. And the more I did it—the yoga, the breathing, the standing there all radiant and free and in front of the ocean—the more I started to feel it. I was pretty sure it was happiness.
>
> I giggled. Like Sarah.
>
> And I can't be certain, but I think the ocean was singing to me as I danced in front of her. Shhhhh, shhhhh, she kept whispering. I felt so big, and so small. I felt like such a miracle.
>
> It's taken me a long time to figure out who I've been all along.[3]

When I first started sharing my story, looking for someone to support me in the process, one of the pieces of feedback I got surprised me. One editor said, "It would be nice if the story had a better resolution." I took that to mean that it would be nice if the story ended with an apology from the man who had done all that damage in my life, or if some new man had come along to resolve my "problem" of being alone and having to start over.

At first I thought, *Yes, sure, wouldn't that be nice if that was the way the story was resolved?* But then I realized that, actually, I'd resolved my story exactly the way I wanted it to resolve. I had written the ending the way I wanted it written. The ending of the story was about *me*—not about getting a new husband or a nicer boyfriend.

The idea that stories have to wrap up perfectly in order to wrap up at all is not only untrue, it often keeps us from finding the deeper, better resolution. Even when the facts of our story can't change, our thoughts and feelings about the story can. Usually, that is more than enough. Maybe the resolution we're looking for is closer than we think.

No matter what story you are looking to resolve in your life right now—the story about your purpose on the planet, the story about what's going to happen with a loved one who is ill, or the story about when you're going to finally meet "the one" and get hitched, don't forget what you have already learned and know to be true:

- You are the protagonist in your own story. The resolution will be about *you* and nobody else.
- Your narrator voice knows everything you need to know because it knows *you* better than anybody else does.
- While the external problems in our stories don't always perfectly resolve, the internal problems can and do.

Yes, we often wait for long periods of time while a story decides how it wants to evolve and when it's going to end. The waiting can be excruciating and terrifying. So many factors are out of our hands. But putting a few words on the page will always show us where our agency lies: with our thoughts and feelings. It will always bring us back to what we know is true: the facts. It will remind us what the story is *really* about: our transformation. And as we consider how we'd like to participate in the ending, a nuanced, beautiful, deep, and true resolution will eventually come.

## Living toward the Resolution

Melody Miles is a beautiful young woman who came to me because she wanted help picking up the pieces of her life, and she thought writing might be a way to do that. Melody is not the person you'd expect to be "picking up the pieces of her life," since she'd been holding the pieces of her own life and the lives of others together for years as a staffer/program officer/global expert at the Bill and Melinda Gates Foundation.

But somehow, while she was working for one of the most powerful couples on the planet, Melody's mother became very sick, and her husband announced he was leaving, and no matter what Melody did, she could not keep her personal life from falling apart. So eventually, Melody asked to take time away.

This is when Melody ended up on my doorstep. She told me, as a handful of my clients do, that she wasn't there to get a big publishing contract or sell a bunch of books or become famous. She just wanted to write her story and understand it better. I affirmed Melody's decision and told her I was glad she was there. It's a significant investment of time and resources to work with me one-on-one, so I knew she was committed to the process, wherever it took her.

We started the day as we always do, with Melody telling me a little bit about her story. I'm always listening for elements of the story that I know we'll want to revisit later, so I took notes. As she recounted the events of the past twelve months to me, I scribbled down a few things.

The first one was that although she identified as a Christian, Melody said, "I became a Christian because I thought life wouldn't hurt so bad. I was wrong about that." The other thing she said that stood out to me came at the end of a handful of stories she recounted about her travels overseas. She had seen some tragedy and devastation in the world and was on the front lines with other people who were formulating ways to help.

As Melody shared the details of these experiences with me, she wasn't even consciously making a connection between them and the tragedy and devastation in her own life—or at least, not that she shared out loud. Regarding the suffering of the world, she said, "The thing I'm learning is that you can't fix suffering without feeling it first." To me, that line was narrator voice. So I wrote it down.

The other thing I took notes on as we talked that morning was a list of the big questions she was asking. Remember, questions are what drive great stories and great writing, so as Melody listed these questions she was asking herself during these uncertain times, I scribbled them down:

- Is it possible to feel suffering and joy at the same time?
- Do my head and my heart have to live in conflict with one another?
- Can I learn from a broken heart as much as (or more than) I've learned from power and money and influence?

The final thing that stood out to me as she spoke was the

transformation she was looking for. Remember, stories require transformations, so if you can get clear on the transformation you're after, charting the path gets easier. Melody clearly articulated to me that she wanted to move from saving the souls of the world to saving her own soul. She wanted to believe that being herself was as important as being responsible. And she wanted to go from dreaming small dreams to believing anything was possible.

I'm only sharing with you a fraction of what Melody shared with me that day, with her permission. Melody's book (as of the time I write this) has not yet been published—although I believe it can and will be, if that's what she desires. She doesn't have a huge platform. She is not a celebrity, a VIP, or an Instagram influencer. What she does have is a deep well of wisdom, as we all do.

Now that I knew these three things about Melody—the transformation she was seeking, the questions driving it, and where the story was headed—we could move to the floor and start mapping out her book.

We spent the next few hours sprawled on my living room floor with note cards. I helped her get all of her stories and narrator wisdom and questions in place. And when we got to the end of the process, around 3 p.m., she stood back and looked for the first time at what would soon be her book.

"There's my book," she said, beaming at me. In front of her were rows of notecards, each labeled with a tentative chapter title and a card that read "Chapter 1" or "Chapter 2" or whatever. There were twelve rows, a great number of chapters, with various numbers of cards in each row.

What happened next is important. As Melody looked down at the note cards in front of her—*her* stories and life experiences and the little pieces of wisdom that had come out of *her* mouth, she realized something. She realized that there were notecards in every "chapter" of the book except the last one. We had titled this final column "You can always change your life," the words she had said earlier that morning verbatim, which did a great job of signifying the final change she was looking to make. But for now, the "contents" of that chapter stood empty. No resolution yet.

I told Melody what I always tell writers when they point out how the last "chapter" of their book doesn't have any content yet. It doesn't have any content yet because it hasn't happened yet. And it hasn't happened yet because you're still living *toward* the resolution.

What Melody did next did not surprise me. She didn't go back to work after our time together. She didn't even go home. Instead, she decided she'd spend the next year or so traveling around the world, on her own, figuring out what she wanted for her life. Why? Because she needed to discover a way to save her own soul before trying to save the world, because she wanted to care less about being responsible and more about being herself, and because she wanted to believe anything was possible.

But above all, Melody knew that she—and only she—could change her life. She had discovered her story was still being written, and she, the narrator of her life, was the only one who could direct where it would go from here.

Here's what I'd like you to take away from Melody's bravery. When you begin to write down the elements of your life, don't be shocked if it completely shifts your direction. It will change the ending. When we change the way we look at the events that have taken and are taking place in our life, it can't help but change our reactions and our responses. I've hinted at this many times already, but I haven't directly said it: *the words you put on paper* will *change the ending of the story.* It's impossible for them not to.

Change might not happen overnight. It might not happen in

the first four days you write. It might not be an immediately positive shift—like waving some kind of magic fairy wand. Sometimes things have to get dismantled before they can be properly put back together. But change is the inevitable promise of looking at our stories from a narrator's perspective. It is the promise of participating in the resolution. This is the power of writing it down.

## The Anatomy of an Ending

The chaos and confusion and bleakness that comes right before any story's resolution is a technique used by storytellers everywhere. This is the moment right before the ending of the sports film you loved where the team you've been following is about to make a free throw shot and their worst shooter is on the free throw line.

This technique is powerful not only because it keeps a reader's or viewer's suspense, but also because it mimics real life. Often, we're standing on the precipice of a "happy ending," of something new and exciting right at the moment when things seem like they're falling apart.

This is the moment when we can't see the hope of resolution. All we can see is that we've been digging for weeks and have nothing to show for it. All we can see is the metaphorical free throw shot clock ticking down and our *worst* shooter poised to attempt a free throw.

Since I've spent the last ten years of my life listening to people's personal stories for a living, I can tell you that this strange phenomenon is present with a remarkable predictability. Maybe you're in this kind of position in your life right now. Maybe you're staring at the terrible diagnosis, or the loss of your children, or the loss of a job and the resulting financial strain on your family. Whatever it is, things are bleak. You're waiting for a hopeful resolution. I wonder if it will help you to know that when writers come to work with me to map out their personal stories, they are almost *always* standing in this kind of chaotic, unresolved moment.

Writing is a beautiful and tender invitation to stay with the story. To reimagine the ending. To play a role in shaping it. Imagine: you get to participate in how this all resolves.

For those writers, and for you, the challenge is this: can you stay in the story for long enough to contribute to the resolution? Or, because it's hard to hold space between questions and answers, have you "written" the ending before it's happened? Have you given up on yourself? Have you decided your teammate is going to miss the shot before he's even thrown it?

If you think of your life as a story, consider that maybe all is not lost, but that you're just standing in the "all is lost" moment right now.[4] How does it change the way you see it? You are the only hero of your story. You are the protagonist. Only you can decide what happens next.

I know it's painful to sit in the middle of a story that seems like it may never resolve. I know what it feels like to believe that you've tried everything, and nothing is working. I also know you are stronger than you ever imagined.

Don't give up and go home just yet. We're almost finished.

CHAPTER 13

# The Beauty of the Writing Life

## How this tool brings more beauty, meaning, and pleasure into your life

I worked with a client named Sarah who wants to write a book. Sarah is one of the wealthiest people I have ever known, and yet she told me she wants to write a book so that she can finally contribute something of value. I couldn't help but stop her to talk about that phrase: *contribute something of value.* Sarah is generous with her wealth—more generous than I could ever dream to be if we're talking about dollar amounts. I had to ask: didn't she feel like she was already *adding value*?

"I wish I could let everyone experience the kind of wealth I have experienced," she said. "It's fine. I'm grateful for it. I love to share. But money is just money. What I really want to share with the world is a piece of myself. "

The great beauty of the writing life is that it draws you back to the page again and again and again to remind you how valuable you are. To remind you that, no matter how much money is or is not in your bank account, you have something to contribute.

I keep thinking about the video message I got from my friend and client, Amy, a few weeks ago. She and I tooled around with a book idea a few years ago. She teaches people how to deliver speeches for a living, so I thought it would be a good idea for her to put everything she knows about public speaking into a book. We outlined the book together, and she was slowly working on it in the background of her life, wondering what all of us wonder about our words. What would happen with them? Were they worth the time and effort?

Then, out of nowhere, something small Amy did with her husband and two young daughters caught some unexpected media attention. After their tiny town of Newberg, Oregon suffered a few tragic deaths by suicide in a short period of time, Amy's family responded by making simple, encouraging signs to place around the neighborhood. The signs said things in plain text like, "You matter" and "Don't give up." Amy drove around the neighborhood, asking friends and neighbors to display the signs in their yards.

Over the years, the family received unbelievable feedback about how these simple words had uplifted passersby—helping them get through a tough divorce, or cope with a lost job, or, in one scenario, reconsider a planned suicide. Friends and family started asking Amy if she could print some of the same signs for them, so they could place them in their neighborhoods, too. Slowly but surely, the "Don't give up" movement ended up all over the state, the country, and eventually, the world.[1]

Then, one day in May of 2019, the movement caught national media attention.

When this happened, Amy got an unexpected email in her inbox. The email was from a New York publishing house, asking her if she had ever considered writing a book. She immediately called to tell me the news. This was when I told her that before she engaged too deeply with this publisher, she should probably think about finding an agent. Ask and you shall receive, I suppose, because before the day was over, Amy had an email from a New York agent in her inbox. Now Amy—from Newberg, Oregon—is writing a book called *Signs of Hope*.

I tell you this story knowing that many of you have absolutely *no* desire to write or publish a book and also, that a handful of you might pray something similar happens to you. But knowing Amy didn't set out to write a book, I tell you her story to remind you that *no matter who you are or where you live or what you do for a living, you have something to say that matters*. Your words—even three simple words like DON'T GIVE UP—are working to create a new world.

As I sit here this morning with the sun gently coming in through the half-translucent shade, I think of another friend who sent me a text last week. This friend doesn't plan to publish anything. In fact, because so much of her life has been lived in the spotlight, it feels crucial at this time for her to keep her words to herself. She is creating a little privacy for herself, a sacred space where she doesn't have to perform for anyone. A space where she can just be herself.

I challenged her to write a love letter to herself. It sounds cheesy, sure, but I told her that the world is full of people who love her more than she seems to love herself. I thought it might be a nice exercise for her to see that no matter how much other people love you, if you don't love yourself, you'll feel empty. So she wrote the letter and when I asked her how it went she nodded and shrugged her shoulders. That was it.

Then, last week, I got a message from her. She said she had woken up feeling kind of down and was having a hard time getting any writing done. So instead of writing, she ended up scrolling through what she's written already. That's when she saw it: the little love note to herself. One small line at the end of her love letter caught her attention. It was spaced out so that it hardly seemed like it was connected to the rest of the letter, a tiny little postscript. This part read, "P.S. Don't forget you're beautiful."

When we make even a small commitment to put our words on paper, we never know what might happen. But one possibility is this: our voices will carry us and come back to us from the past. They will remind us who we are. Again and again and again.

## Metabolize Your Life

Through the gift of the written word, you now have a tool to digest and metabolize all that happens to you. Imagine a world in which you didn't have a digestive system, and you kept eating and eating food for fuel, but your body couldn't break down the food very well, or it couldn't grab the nutrients you need, so it would all get stuck inside of you. Eventually, your body would become a toxic environment, where what was meant for your flourishing turned into poison. You'd be sick all the time.

Our digestive systems don't just digest food. In fact, sometimes our stomachs are called "the second brain," because unlike any other organ in our body, they can operate independently of the brain.[2] Our stomachs are responsible for our intuition, or "gut" instinct. They house the good bacteria that make up part of our immune system—how foreign invaders are kept from harming us. Our digestive tracts are our first line of defense. What better metaphor could there be for our writing life?

If you do not metabolize your life well through reflectively digesting the "facts" of what has happened to you, even nourishing events can become toxic. If you *do* metabolize your life in a healthy way, you'll be able to process and use for your good even things that are heartbreaking and tragic. Forget the fact that our *personal* lives are filled with heartbreak. We live in a world where we're exposed to heartbreak and tragedy every day. Thanks to the media, we have more of this in front of our eyes than ever before: mass shootings and war and political division and images of death and anguish.

How are we supposed to digest all of it? Does it ever feel like it's just sitting in your system, all poisonous and heavy? Writing is a tool you can use for digestion.

Take a minute and think about the last time an event from your life or from the news really bothered you. Maybe it was a fight with your significant other or some new terror you watched unfold on the news. Perhaps it was even an unsettling scene in a TV show that really struck you, and now you can't stop thinking about it. I woke up this morning after a terrible, vivid dream and could not shake the heaviness.

Why do you think your mind keeps bringing up these things, even when you find them uncomfortable or alarming? Is it possible that your brain is trying to tell you something—that there's something in your reaction worth further examination? Writing is a great way to excavate an emotional reaction and find the *why* behind it.

When you exercise the power of language to name how you think and feel about things, those feelings no longer have power over you. They no longer overwhelm you. You no longer have to waste an entire day being distracted and unproductive at work as your mind unconsciously tries to work out a problem your conscious brain won't acknowledge. You can stop and write for five minutes, or ten, or twenty if you need it. You can put some words to what you're feeling. And you can find the relief that comes with knowing that truth.

Connie, who came to one of our Find Your Voice workshops,

told the group she'd been going through a hard time with a friend who was wrapped up in an addiction. This friend would go back and forth between being apologetic and kind, swearing she was going to get sober and change. Then, days later, she'd be back at the casino, gambling and drinking.

To make things even more dramatic, when she got drunk, she'd turn vindictive and cold to Connie. She'd send malicious text messages or sometimes pick up the phone and yell and scream at Connie. She'd even shown up at Connie's house a time or two. Connie hated watching her friend in pain and told us she would do anything to help. But she was stuck. Nothing she was doing was working.

She wrote about the situation with her friend during one of our writing prompts that day. When the twenty minutes was up, I looked over and saw Connie sitting with tears streaming down her face. She looked sad, but strangely resolved. I asked her if she'd like to share what she had discovered. She nodded.

"I realized how sad I am," she said. "But it's not what you think. I'm sad for my friend, sure. I want her to get better. But what makes me even more sad is that I've allowed her to be violent toward me one too many times. She's taking me down with her because I'm letting her. Why would I do that to myself?"

This realization—that she was harming *herself* as much or more than her friend was harming her—was the realization that unhooked Connie from the drama she'd been wrapped in for years now. It was the breaking point for Connie. And it was an incredible relief for her, even before she made any changes. Sometimes it's a relief just to have words for why we feel the way we feel.

Having the words also helps us take positive action toward resolution. In the next writing session, I had Connie write a letter to her friend, explaining what she needed from her. The letter was long and packed with insight, but the best part, in my opinion, was the last line. This was the part that helped Connie get to a new solution. It read, "I need space. I cannot put myself in the way of harm anymore."

Imagine if you knew that you had all the wisdom, all the direction, all the answers you needed buried inside you. If you knew that you could get yourself out of a rut, give yourself brilliant advice, unhook yourself from the drama that has been plaguing you for far too long, what would you do? I'm here to tell you that you *do* have access to these seemingly out-of-reach solutions. You already have the wisdom you need, buried in the stories you are already living.

To get to it, all you have to do is metabolize your life.

## Framing Our Lives

Imagine I brought you into my house and showed you around. Imagine that before we walked inside together, I told you that while you were inside, you really didn't want to miss the ceilings. They were intricately detailed and handcrafted in Italy. I told you that they'd survived countless earthquakes in the LA area and never been impacted. That's how sturdy they were.

Now imagine that as we walked through the house, I kept pointing out the ceilings to you. I'd probably show you how snugly the beams fit together at the corners and share more about the craftsman who made such a masterpiece. We'd walk through the house this way for some time, and then I'd usher you back outside to say goodbye. Now, imagine that when we got outside I asked, "What did you think of the floors?"

You'd be confused. That's because I didn't *frame* the floors for you. I framed the ceiling. Framing is when you direct someone's attention toward a specific detail. As the narrator of your own story, you get to do the framing.

Framing matters because often, we haven't stopped to consider the point of the story. Or perhaps we're not patient enough to ask the question that doesn't yet have an answer. As a result, we're paying attention to the wrong things. We're focused on details that don't matter.

We're staring at the ceiling when the main event is really the floors.

Framing finishes the sentence, "The reason I'm telling you this is because . . ." This is helpful when you're writing because, if you aren't sure of the answer to that question, you had better spend some time thinking about it. If you can't come up with an answer, the detail or story has to go.

Let me ask you a question. How are you framing your life to yourself? Are you paying attention to the wrong things? Are you spending lots of time on things that don't matter?

Writing can help you clear the clutter.

At least three times a week, I have a conversation with someone, somewhere about social media. Most people say they need to use it less, but since it doesn't seem like social media is going anywhere anytime soon, my question is always, "What can social media teach us about how we're framing our lives?"

## The Limits of Writing

It's right and fair for me to list the limits of the writing process here. Writing can't cure cancer, for example. Writing can't bring our loved ones back when they are gone. Writing can't stop something from hurting that simply hurts—losing a spouse, a child, a dream. These things seem to be an inevitable part of the human experience. If anything, writing puts us *in touch* with our human experience, which might make us more aware of the pain. Not less. I wish I could tell you writing is a magic pill. This book would sell better. But that would be untrue.

My friend Beth lost her husband, Alex, about eight weeks before she was meant to give birth to their first child, a son. When I heard the news, I cancelled all my plans, got on a plane, and flew from LAX to Nashville to be with her. Losing Alex was the biggest tragedy of my life to date, and that doesn't even touch what it was and is for Beth. Any tragedy I've experienced pales in comparison to hers.

For the first few days I was there with her, she barely spoke, and when she did, it was usually the same phrases over and over again ("Where is he?" and "When is he coming back?"). But slowly, as the facts of the situation started to sink in, and she came back to herself, memories of Alex would come back to her—things he'd said or done. Friends flocked to the house in crowds, and we told stories about Alex, talked about what we loved about him, and laughed at the things he would have said if he had been there.

At one point, Beth asked me if I would start writing these things down—the song he made up for the dog at dinner, the time he made up a Jazzercise routine in the living room. Your brain on grief doesn't remember things very well, so every now and then, I sent her little notes to remind her of what people had said so she could go back and reread them later. Over time, Beth started doing this too—writing down her thoughts and feelings—about the process of finishing her last trimester and giving birth to their son.

Her notes were broken fragments, and appropriately so. Our writing reflects where we are in our ability to process things. Over time, they became this little collection of memories. They do not bring Alex back. They do not have that power. But over time, our words do tend to bring the smallest measure of comfort in the midst of something that is otherwise comfortless.

Writing isn't for everyone in the midst of trauma and grief.

But when your heart pulls you to write things down, it's often an invitation to some measure of healing and relief. When the words come, the writing life draws us back to the one thing that can never be taken away, regardless of our unexplainable losses: our voice. Writing is not a cure-all. But it does invite us to reconnect with our memory, to make meaning of our unique experience and sometimes to speak the truth we didn't feel we could speak anywhere else.

Over time, as we metabolize, we *do* find a way to carry the most important pieces of our experiences with us—and to leave behind the parts that are weighing us down. If we're lucky, we can even find small, unexpected bits of nourishment in a sea of unbearable loss.

CHAPTER 14

# The Gift You Leave Behind

## How words make you a person of influence

It's crazy to think how much we try to remember that we cannot remember. Our lives pass quickly, and most of what we do on a given day fades into the background of our brains like white noise. Can you remember what you did last Thursday? What about a year ago today? You might be able to take a guess at where you were, who you were with, or what general things you were doing—but do you really *remember*?

What do you remember about your life? When was the last time you felt joyful? What about devastated? Research shows you're much more likely to be able to answer the second question than the first. Negative emotions carve deep ruts in our brains and are memorized by our bodies so they can be replayed over and over and over again. Positive emotions like joy and peace and love don't always have the same impact.

Do you want to get to the end of your life and remember only the negative? What parts do you want to remember?

What we write down is what we remember. It's like a time capsule in a way, a lifeline back to the best parts of ourselves. A little popcorn trail of words we can follow so that we never lose sight of the path we're on. Words help us see ourselves more clearly. They help us remember who we are and what we're here for. They help others remember us, too.

Our words become our legacy.

This is why I'm writing this book. It's why anyone writes a book. The book itself may be nothing. It may be a long-winded road that leads to nowhere. It may be nothing spectacular. This is the risk we take with our lives, and this is the risk we take with our pens. It may be nothing much in the end. But you'd better believe I'm going to try to make it a little bit of something.

This is why you, too, dream of putting words down on paper without having any idea where they could take you. Because words will help us remember the parts of ourselves we have long forgotten. Because words guide us and guide those who come behind us. Because for all the energy and effort and love and passion we put into this world, words are the most lasting thing we get to leave behind.

## Why Am I Still Writing?

It's so easy to give up on our writing. I hear this expressed not only by those who set off on this path as a means of self-discovery but also by published authors who have seen massive success. The easy thing to do would be to walk away, give up, leave the writing for the "real" writers who were "born to do it," whoever they are.

So why do we keep pushing ahead? What am I supposed to tell a writer when they send me an email that says they want to give up?

I tell that writer about the private diary of Anne Frank, a young Jewish girl who lived and died during World War II. The words in that book—which have now been read almost ubiquitously by generations of students—were written by a thirteen-year-old girl who had no idea what she was writing while she was writing it. She even makes a comment in the journal to that effect.

> Writing in a diary is a really strange experience for someone like me. Not only because I've never written anything before, but also because it seems to me that later on neither I nor anyone else will be interested in the musings of a thirteen-year old school girl. Oh well, it doesn't matter. I feel like writing.[1]

Catch the irony here. This is a book that has sold more than 30 million copies and has been translated into 70 languages. But did Anne Frank know her words would be read that widely? Or did she just *feel* like writing? Despite the challenges that present themselves in the process, if we can get over this idea that we need our words to be read by millions (or that we're terrified of who will read them), I think *we* also *feel* like writing.

Most of us, when we get over our need to be important to the world, realize how important we already *are*. Then, and only then, do the words and ideas that have always been trying to be expressed through us finally come.

I worked with a client who lost his wife tragically in a freak crime in Indianapolis. They had a fifteen-month-old son, and she was thirteen weeks pregnant with their daughter at the time. So Davey lost two loved ones that day—his wife and his daughter. After Amanda's death, Davey found stacks and stacks of Amanda's journals and started reading through her entries. They were a relic of her. A little treasure left behind in the wake of unthinkable tragedy.

This is the power of putting our words down on paper. It's a tiny part of us we get to leave behind when we're gone.

If the thought of someone reading your journals after you're gone terrifies you the way it does me, you'll appreciate this part of the story. During the flight home after my meeting with Davey, I texted my sister and made her promise that if anything ever happened to me, she would destroy every journal I'd ever written. I was half-joking, but also thinking about what a remarkable person Amanda was and how my postmortem journal entries might not be quite so flattering.

When I got home, I went straight to my desk drawer and started thumbing through old journals, thinking about what I had written over time and what it would say about me. One entry I found made me lose my breath.

It was from a time in my life I've talked about quite a bit in this book—when I was stuck in an abusive and manipulative relationship. For the most part, I didn't journal while I was in that relationship. I didn't feel the liberty to speak freely, and I was terrified what would happen if he ever discovered what I wrote. But on a page that was filled primarily with a grocery list and a to-do list and some random doodling, there was a tiny sentence scribbled so you could barely read it.

"I never knew love could feel so much like hate."

To be honest, I'm not sure if I was saying that he hated me, or I hated him. Or maybe some of both. What is visceral to me, and the reason I'm including this story here—along with Davey's—is that words can be like time capsules. What is true at a certain point in time doesn't necessarily *stay* true. As our words evolve, so do we. As we evolve, so do our words. And as we read back over words we've written, we get to see how far we've come.

If your journals were left behind after you leave this place, what would they say? The words we use say a lot about us. I don't say this to make you feel ashamed or to terrify you out of an honest journal entry. I say it to remind you that often, the extraordinary is found in the obvious, everyday moments of our lives—the musings of a thirteen-year-old girl, for example. The thoughts and prayers of a devoted wife and mother in Indianapolis. The tiny gem of wisdom beneath a grocery list. I say this to remind you that what seems ordinary about your life might just be more worthy of a long, loving look than you ever imagined.

If you don't ever write down the words, how will you know?

## On Having Influence

In every generation, we make choices that seem permissible at minimum and perhaps even good at the time. It isn't until later that we look back and wonder what on earth we were thinking. There are obvious examples like the Holocaust, but there are also simpler ones like the one I'm about to share with you.

One of those things, for my generation, will be "influencer culture." There will come a time when we look back and we wonder what we were thinking when we elevated certain people to hero status, VIP status, celebrity status—whatever you want to call it—simply because they had some sort of blue check mark next to their name on Instagram. The entire thing is absurd when you really think about it.

To be clear, wanting to be an "influencer" or a "person of influence" isn't a bad thing. When you really listen to people, you'll hear almost everyone express the desire to have an impact on the world. This might look different for you than it does for me, but none of us want to leave this earth and be forgotten. Even the most hardened criminals express a twisted sense of doing what they did so that nobody would ever forget them.

But the question remains, *What does it mean to be a person of influence?* I'm afraid that somewhere along the way, we've gotten the answer to this question all wrong.

Take a minute and think about a person who has had a profound influence on your life. Maybe it's a parent or a sibling or a teacher you had in high school. Or maybe, for you, it's not someone you know personally at all. Perhaps you've been influenced by someone who actually *is* in the spotlight in a literal way—a celebrity or public figure like Julia Cameron or Michelle Obama (two women who've had a profound influence on me).

To influence someone means to have a transformative effect on their lives. To be a player in their story. If you think about a person who has had *influence* in your life, I imagine you'll find this is true. They've had an effect on your character, development, or behavior. By this definition, I'm sure that some Instagram "influencers" are truly influential. But my guess is that the sad majority of them aren't influencing anyone to do much more than feel bad about themselves, or to envy a false reality.

What's even more tragic is that those of us who *know* this to be true still, in some odd way, aspire to become like those "influencers." We find ourselves mimicking them, perfecting and refining our photos and captions, spinning the story of our lives until what we're presenting to the world is light years away from our actual reality. We feel disconnected from ourselves, we feel disconnected from the world around us, and we feel more and more disconnected from our authentic power. This is the only "influence" some of us will ever have. Tragic.

The good news is, words give us back our power. And if we can learn to use them to tell the truth, we move beyond the childish need to get attention and likes and comments on social media, and we actually *become* a person of influence. That first kind of influence might seem appealing—to have a lot of people paying attention. But it's only superficial. The second kind of influence focuses less on how many people are paying attention and more on the message we're offering. How is it shaping them? How is it shaping *us*?

Would you rather your influence be wide or deep?

If you want to be a person of influence—if you want

something from your life to remain behind—you are going to have to look beyond growing your "platform" online. Platforms grow when they grow, and they die when they die. Platforms can be yanked out from beneath you in a matter of seconds. I know because it has happened to me, and I've watched it happen to clients. I've also watched clients all but sell their souls to save their platforms—to their own destruction and detriment.

We aren't built to stand on stages. The spotlight is not what we really want. What we want is to stand foot-to-foot with another human being, palm pressed to warm palm, and to look them in the eyes. Writing will help you do that.

For some of you, it will be the first time.

Words are an excellent way to connect to the humanity inside you and to find the humanity in others. But not just any words will do. The words must be simple, they must be human, they must be *yours*, and they must be true. This is the gift expressive writing will give to you, to your family, and to the generations that come after you. Sure, it will take some time. Yes, the blank page is rather frustratingly dramatic. Of course you will want to give up a thousand times along the way.

But what could possibly be more worth it?

## The Gift of Your Words

There are so few things that live on after we're gone from this earth. Our physical possessions get divided up among family members and next of kin. Our money gets passed on as an inheritance and eventually disappears, too. Hopefully we leave a legacy of love, inspiration, or community behind, but how can we be sure that the torches we carried in this lifetime will be carried by those who follow? Words help us do this.

Most people don't know that as John Steinbeck wrote *East of Eden*, arguably one of the greatest novels of the twentieth century, he kept himself motivated by writing private letters to his editor, Pat. These letters were later compiled and published as a work called *Journal of a Novel*. It's a short work, divided up by dates rather than chapters, just like a journal would be. Steinbeck writes candidly about the writing process, his hopes for the book, his hesitations about himself as the author, and even the occasional life detail that has nothing to do with the book, like how he goes to a department store to look at grass rugs with his wife.

It's the perfect depiction of the writing life: mundane and obvious, while at the same time complex and profound.

Although this piece of writing by Steinbeck is probably the least known of all his works, his words have left a lasting impression on me, on my team, on our clients, and on anyone who joins us for workshops. His words are a beacon of hope for us as they are reminding us what to focus on and why what we do matters:

> I am choosing to write this book to my sons. They are little boys now and they will never know what they came from through me unless I tell them. . . . if the book is addressed to them, it is for good reason. I want them to know how it was, I want to tell them directly, and perhaps by speaking directly to them I shall speak directly to other people.[2]

The only way we will ever have a shot at speaking to other people is if we start by speaking to ourselves. To our kids. To the people who are closest to us. To the ones we love the most. You might find yourself feeling like it is too tender and personal a thing to do—to share the most vulnerable details of your life. To that I say, those are the only words I want to read. They're the only ones that matter.

Forget growing a platform. This practice will grow your heart.

## Shape the World

Not only are words the legacy we leave behind, but words shape the world we live in. For better or worse, I grew up reciting the Pledge of Allegiance every single morning at the start of school. We also read and even memorized parts of the Hebrew Scriptures as a part of an evangelical Christian community. I can still recite almost the entire first chapter of the New Testament book of James, which is probably around 1500 words.

As a family, we read *Berenstain Bears* and *Frog and Toad* and *Amelia Bedelia* and eventually I read *The Babysitter's Club* on my own and *The Chronicles of Narnia*. These are the words that carved the superhighway of neural pathways in my brain. They helped shape my viewpoint and understanding of the world. You can probably get a pretty good understanding of who I am and how I grew up simply by knowing the words I read.

The words that shaped my world are different than the words that shaped yours. Have you spent any time thinking about what words have shaped yours? Maybe for you it was the words of Mahatma Gandhi that you read nightly before bed. Perhaps it was the Koran or the Torah. Maybe you memorized Abraham Lincoln's Gettysburg Address or the Catechism of the Catholic Church. Maybe as a family you read poetry by Lord Byron or Mary Oliver or John White.

Or perhaps you can quote practically every line of every Chris Farley movie.

Whoever it was, consider who you might be if it weren't for their words. Now consider that the very words you hold close to your chest could have been written from the monotony of someone's daily life. While they worked at the post office or at Pizza Hut. While they sold electronics at Radio Shack. While they lived in tiny apartments in New York City or the-middle-of-nowhere

Iowa. While they went through break-ups or before they made dinner for their families or while they traveled across the country in a van.

It's a very simple thing, shaping the world we live in. It starts with us. It starts at home. It starts with the people we love most. It's not the stuff of glamour, but make no mistake: words shape who we are and who we become.

## Shaping the World and Saving Your Own Life

It's a lofty thing to talk about—*shaping the world.* It's an important conversation; a responsibility we have, I believe, to leave the communities we're part of better than how we found them. To make sure that the impact we have is a positive one in this lifetime. To think critically and carefully about what serves the greater good, as much or more than what serves our personal interests. And yet I need to emphasize (and reemphasize) how even shaping the world starts with saving our own lives.

Remember the man I told you about back in chapter 5—Robert—who literally saved his own life with his words? His story is a perfect example of the power of writing it down. It demonstrates beautifully how the written word works to shape us first, and then the ripple effect moves beyond us to shape the broader world.

I cannot help but think about how, as I've written this book, so much has changed. Not as a result of *my* words but simply because our world is constantly changing, whether we like it or not. Our words get to play a role in the change—even if it's simply that they force us to pay attention.

This year, a global pandemic unfolded, which has in turn shifted the way we live. The pandemic has left in its wake economic difficulty that still can't be measured. In the midst of some of the greatest communal uncertainty I've experienced in my lifetime, a black man named George Floyd was murdered by police officers in Minneapolis. And while he was certainly not the first black man to experience this tragic and unjust fate, it seems that his death (or perhaps the graphic footage from all different angles) touched a wound for our country in a new way.

White people who weren't paying attention are now paying attention. Black people are being forced to grieve—*again*—a 400-year history of oppression. They are feeling a collective and appropriate rage. We are in a long-awaited revolution. Depending on who you are, this could seem unsettling. Or it could seem hopeful. Or it could be some combination of many things. Regardless, the world is changing, and our words are contributing—whether we're aware or not.

Meanwhile, my husband and I are about to welcome a baby girl into our lives. Speaking of *change*, the changes in our world are not just global but personal. Life keeps spinning and moving along. And words help us not only *track* the change but also *participate* in them. They help us not only define the world we live in but also contribute to it in a meaningful way.

I cannot help but also think about a friend who is no longer with us. I was helping him with a book before he tragically passed away. Now his book won't be finished the way we thought it would.

He was writing on the disease of addiction—a way to tell his own story and also raise awareness around the addiction pandemic that has become a national health crisis in the last decade. One of the most memorable things he ever told me was a counterpoint to the common idea that addicts need to reach "rock bottom" before we can ever have a chance of saving them. He would rant, "Addiction is the *only disease* where we wait until it's at its highest level of acuity before we treat it." He contended that waiting until an addict reached "rock bottom" before offering intervention was like knowing there was an asteroid headed toward earth—and that it was going to split the earth in two—and doing nothing about it.

He's right. Why would we wait until things are *as bad as they can possibly get* before we dig into the words that have the power to change our personal realities, the communities that we live in, and the world around us?

If not now, then when?

As I consider the words my friend shared with me while he was still here, I cannot help but think about the great pain and the great gift that writing offers. You cannot write your words without living them. You cannot share your words without writing them. The stakes are high. It can be daunting at times. But buried in our words is wisdom that can save lives.

Through our words, we get to architect the kind of world we want to live in. Perhaps, through our words, we can lighten the load of our own suffering. And if that's all our words ever do—isn't it enough? And perhaps, by some miracle, we can lighten the load for someone else through our words. Perhaps we can remind them what it feels like to be human. Perhaps our words can move them to a deeper level of compassion. And perhaps, by that simple magic, we get to leave a little bit of us behind us when we go.

All of this through the simple power of writing it down.

Acknowledgments

Most people think writing is a solitary endeavor. What they don't realize is that behind every book and every author is a village of people that make it possible for the words to exist that you are reading now.

For me, that village of people includes my team at Find Your Voice—Annie, Ashley, Josh, Ryan, and Braden. Thanks for making work fun and for taking great care of our authors so I could get my own book written.

Thank you to my editor, Stephanie, who was (serendipitously) also editor of the very first book I ever published. Thanks for believing in me and my writing from the beginning.

Thank you to my agent, Bryan, for seeing in this book what I saw in it and for helping me find a home for it.

To my clients, who trust me with the most important messages and words of their lives. Thank you for sharing yourself with me. It's because of you that I come back to this work again and again.

To my husband, Matt, who has been a steady support and cheerleader for me as I've written these words.

To you, my reader. It's *with* you, as much as for you, that I keep coming back to the gift of writing again and again. Here's to the many beautiful and healing words we have yet to write.

# Notes

## Chapter 1: Something to Express

1. The information I'm about to share with you in the paragraphs that follow is an incredibly simplistic rendering of what I've learned from many different sources, including Dr. Joe Dispenza's *Breaking the Habit of Being Yourself: How to Lose Your Mind and Create a New One* (Hay House, Inc., 2012)—an excellent read (when you finish this book, of course).
2. I first came across Dr. Pennebaker's work through his obscure but fascinating book, *The Secret Life of Pronouns: What Our Words Say About Us* (Bloomsbury Press, 2011), which details how the pronouns we use can tell us about our emotional and mental state, and how we see ourselves in the world.
3. James Pennebaker, *Writing to Heal: A Guided Journal for Recovering from Trauma and Emotional Upheaval* (Center for Journal Therapy, Inc., 2013), 9.
4. Pennebaker, 7.

## Chapter 2: But I'm Not a Writer

1. Denise Schmandt-Besserat, "The Evolution of Writing," University of Texas, January 25, 2014, https://sites.utexas.edu/dsb/tokens/the-evolution-of-writing/.
2. "Double Jeopardy: How Third Grade Reading Skills and Poverty Influence High School Graduation," The Annie E. Casey Foundation, January 1, 2012, https://www.aecf.org/resources/double-jeopardy/.
3. Andrew Sum, Ishwar Khatiwada, Joseph McLaughlin with Sheila Palma, "The Consequences of Dropping Out of High School: Joblessness and Jailing for High School Dropouts and

the High Cost for Taxpayers," Center for Labor Market Studies, Northeastern University, Boston, MA, October 2009, https://www.prisonpolicy.org/scans/The_Consequences_of_Dropping_Out_of_High_School.pdf.
4. tbd
5. Qtd. in George Bainton, *The Art of Authorship* (New York: D. Appleton and Company, 1890), 87–88.
6. I'm taking this term, "expressive writing," from Dr. James Pennebaker's and Dr. Joshua Smyth's book *Opening Up by Writing It Down* (New York: The Guilford Press, 2016). This is the type of writing that helps us heal and understand our lives, as opposed to the kind of writing you do when you make a to-do list.

### Chapter 3: The Sacred Act of Making Space

1. "Mary Oliver: Listening to the World," interview by Krista Tippett, *On Being*, February 5, 2015, https://onbeing.org/programs/mary-oliver-listening-to-the-world-jan2019/.
2. Virginia Woolf, *A Room of One's Own* (New York: Harcourt, 1929).

### Chapter 4: The Drama of the Blank Page

1. Billy Collins, "Aristotle," *Sailing Alone Around the Room* (New York: Random House, 2011), 132.

### Chapter 6: Stories Worth Telling

1. Pennebaker, *Opening Up by Writing It Down*, 23.
2. Stefanie P. Spera, Eric D. Buhrfeind, and James W. Pennebaker, "Expressive Writing and Coping with Job Loss," *The Academy of Management Journal* 37, no. 3, June 1994, https://www.jstor.org/stable/256708?seq=1.
3. Ibid.
4. Dr. Bessel Van Der Kolk explores this in *The Body Keeps the Score*, addressing how if we only talk, we're accessing one part of our brain, and we miss out on what the other parts of our brain have to teach us about ourselves. How do we access these other parts of our brain? Yoga, meditation, experiential therapy, neurofeedback—and of course, writing.

### Chapter 7: Getting Stuck (and Unstuck)

1. Ryan Pinkham, "80% of Smartphone Users Check Their Phones Before Brushing Their Teeth . . . And Other Hot Topics," *Constant Contact*, https://blogs.constantcontact.com/smartphone-usage-statistics/.

### Chapter 8: Write Now, Edit Later

1. *The Office*, season 7, episode 10, "China," directed by Charles McDougall, written by Greg Daniels, developed for American television by Halsted Stevens, featuring Steve Carell, Rainn Wilson, and John Krasinski, aired December 2, 2010, on NBC.

### Chapter 9: Becoming Your Own Narrator

1. Chelsea Wakefield, *Negotiating the Inner Peace Treaty: Becoming the Person You Were Born to Be* (Bloomington, IN: Balboa Press, 2012).
2. If you haven't already, please read the excellent depiction of what happens when we think of our lives as stories in Donald Miller's book, *A Million Miles in a Thousand Years*.
3. Jared B. Torre and Matthew D. Lieberman, "Putting Feelings into Words: Affect Labeling as Implicit Emotion Regulation," *Emotion Review* 10, no. 2, April 2018, https://www.scn.ucla.edu/pdf/Torre(2018)ER.pdf.
4. Arash Javanbakht and Linda Saab, "What Happens in the Brain When We Feel Fear," SmithsonianMag.com, October 27, 2017, https://www.smithsonianmag.com/science-nature/what-happens-brain-feel-fear-180966992/.
5. Pennebaker, *Opening Up*, 88. Emphasis mine.
6. Pennebaker, *Opening Up*, 135.
7. Pennebaker, *Opening Up*, 136.

### Chapter 10: The Passage of Time

1. Dispenza, *Breaking the Habit of Being Yourself*, 71.
2. Ibid.
3. Pennebaker, *Opening Up*, 94.
4. "The Five Stages to Successful Behavior Change," *Cecelia*

*Health*, April 18, 2019. https://www.ceceliahealth.com/blog/2016/1/20/the-five-stages-to-successful-behavior-change.

## Chapter 11: Write It like a Love Letter

1. Pennebaker, *Opening Up by Writing It Down*, 10.
2. Kathy Benjamin, "60% of People Can't Go 10 Minutes Without Lying," *Mental Floss*, May 7, 2012, https://www.mentalfloss.com/article/30609/60-people-cant-go-10-minutes-without-lying.
3. Lucia Peters, "This Is the Number of Secrets the Average Human Can Actually Keep, According to Science," *Bustle*, May 30, 2017, https://www.bustle.com/p/this-is-the-number-of-secrets-the-average-human-can-actually-keep-according-to-science-61014.
4. Grant Hilary Brenner, MD, "The Secrets You Keep Are Hurting You—Here's How," *Psychology Today*, January 22, 2019, https://www.psychologytoday.com/us/blog/experimentations/201901/the-secrets-you-keep-are-hurting-you-heres-how.
5. Pennebaker, *Opening Up by Writing It Down*, 41.

## Chapter 12: The Ending That Hasn't Been Written

1. J. D. Vance, *Hillbilly Elegy* (New York: HarperCollins, 2018), 257. Emphasis mine.
2. Barbara Kingsolver, *The Poisonwood Bible* (New York: HarperCollins, 1998), 533.
3. Allison Fallon, *Indestructible* (Morgan James Publishing, 2019), 158.
4. Blake Snyder, *Save the Cat!: The Last Book on Screenwriting You'll Ever Need* (Michael Wiese Productions, 2005).

## Chapter 13: The Beauty of the Writing Life

1. Check out the movement yourself at dontgiveupsigns.com.
2. Society for Neuroscience, "'Second Brain' Neurons Keep Colon Moving," *Science Daily*, May 29, 2018, https://www.sciencedaily.com/releases/2018/05/180529132122.htm.

## Chapter 14: The Gift You Leave Behind

1. Anne Frank, *The Diary of a Young Girl: The Definitive Edition* (New York: Anchor Books, 1996), 5–6.
2. John Steinbeck, *Journal of a Novel: The East of Eden Letters* (New York: The Viking Press, 1969), 4.